JIM STOODLEY'S PRIVATE WAR

This book is dedicated to my wife
Sheila

JIM STOODLEY'S PRIVATE WAR

An Autobiography

Cover design: Jon Pierre Trudeau Stoodley
from an original idea by James A. Stoodley

Printed by Livesey Ltd., Shrewsbury.

James Alfred Stoodley
26 Agar Road, Liverpool, England.

Contents

Introduction

On reading the typescript of *Jim Stoodley's Private War* I could see at once what a fascinating story the author had made of it all, and the illustrations, obviously, greatly added to it.

James Stoodley tells the reader about his most fascinating childhood adventures in a unique flowing manner in what I believe is an unparalleled autobiography from the Second World War.

An extremely brave young man, skilful, errant, as well as cunning, it appears certain that he would have been prepared to give his life to defend his country.

If he had been old enough to serve in the Armed Forces, I would have been surprised if he had not been awarded the Victoria Cross (maybe posthumously).

BRYAN GUINNESS
Second Baron Moyne*

*Lord Moyne died in July 1992

Preface

This is a true story of a young boy who was born in Ludgershall and spent his childhood on Salisbury Plain. World War II is the main subject of this story, set in the beautiful Wiltshire countryside, where he found himself very much involved in that conflict. To respect the privacy of persons in this book, some names have been altered, while others have gracefully permitted the author to use their true names, and accounts, of encounters with Jim Stoodley, from his schooldays until the end of the war.

I am indebted to them, and to Ethel Bowman (*nee* Hersey) and her husband, Gordon, who tirelessly gave so much time on researching old school friends on my behalf.

JIM STOODLEY
1985

Acknowledgements

Very special thanks and deepest appreciation for inspiration and help to the late Lord Moyne and Lady Elisabeth Moyne and the Honourable Desmond Guinness.

My thanks and appreciation to the following:

Reg Ayres, Gordon Barker, Bill Bendall, Alma Brown, Monica Chandler, Des Chandler, Peter Collingson, Cathy Collingson, Pam Curtis, Joy Curtis, Ruth Davies, Eileen Faraghly, Mary Fuzzard, Frank Gamble, Graham Goulder, 'Ookey' Goulder, Charlie Hawkins, Ethel Hersey, Gordon Hersey, Tom Humphries, Lily Isham, Rita Isham, Zilda Long, Betty McGlashen, Jean McKinley, Mr and Mrs Mountain, Harvey Perry, Clive Richards, Eric Richards, Jim Simpson, Derek Saunders, Dita Saunders, John Stoodley, Gerald Stoodley, Jean Thurlow, Ivor Winstone, Roy Winstone, Eddy Wilde, Len Watton, Maude Wilkins and my apologies to the long-suffering Wiltshire and Hampshire Constabulary.

Prologue

The date was 29th August 1985, a beautiful August Bank Holiday Monday. I was approaching Tidworth in the car and ahead on the hill, above Tidworth, stood the trees upon which, nearly forty-two years earlier, I had crash-landed the plane.

I drove up to the top of Tidworth Hill and parked up. I walked up to Spion Kop and looked out across my boyhood playground. In the near distance, Ludgershall, my birthplace. To the right a little, Perham Down. Down below me, Brimstone Bottom. The little house my pal Frank Gamble lived in was gone. I wondered where he was now. A flood of happy memories came back to me. I was now fifty-five years old. The sparkle had left the eyes that had once witnessed the coming of the cream of American manhood, many of whom had not returned to their homeland.

Fields were overgrown with bushes, even trees, where hundreds and hundreds of Shermans, halftracks, jeeps, trucks etc., had smothered the open ground for square miles. Down at Brimstone Bottom I could see a few skeletons of old workshops and barracks, now overgrown with the camouflage of time.

I looked hard, my eyes were greedy for something to feast upon, to remind me of those happy days. I sat down and looked over towards Sidbury Hill and then below on Windmill Hill where I had my hide-out when I was fourteen years old.

Yes! being a youngster in those wartime years was a many-splendoured thing. Every second that had ticked slowly by had now multiplied into two score years. Time gone by was lost forever, but happy memories live on very crisp and vivid in my heart.

If ever I could be granted a wish, it would be to hear the brass bands of the U.S. Army marching from Ludgershall station up the road to Windmill Hill again, and hear the rasp of the Sherman's engine as I belted across the main road at Brimstone Bottom on my way to Collingbourne Woods, but, most of all, it would be to live out my last remaining years in my beloved Wiltshire.

JIM STOODLEY
August, 1985

CHAPTER 1

The Beginnings

I WAS born at 2.30 a.m. on 17th July, 1928, in a violent thunderstorm in Ludgershall, Wiltshire, a small, picturesque village, close to the Hampshire border, seven miles from Andover, and three miles from Tidworth, which was, and still is, a large Army garrison complex.

At the outbreak of war in 1939 there were ten boys and four girls in our family, and when the war started I was eleven years old.

Salisbury Plain was my playground, and I had a great choice of pastimes to choose from. I loved to walk over the Plains, explore the many fir tree plantations, the forests, play around Stonehenge, the castles, the hills, the whole beautiful countryside was mine to enjoy. The coming of this dreadful war changed my life.

With the arrival of the U.S. troops in England in 1942, and subsequently to Wiltshire, I was nearly fourteen years old and when I left school (at which I was average in spelling, history, and particularly athletics which was to stand me in good stead in my future escapades) I started work at the Forestry Commission as a lumberjack assistant, then, after a few months, moved to the Royal Ordnance Depot at Tidworth under the supervision of my father, who was in charge of the Motor Pool section, under Colonel Richland of the U.S. Army S.O.S. Ordnance. Here, in this vast 'Treasure House' was an unlimited wealth of tanks, trucks, cars, jeeps, command vehicles of every description, the U.S. Army knew how to supply its troops, and this was only the beginning.

The whole of Salisbury Plain (which in peacetime years was a green and relatively quiet landscape) was rapidly becoming a vast arsenal of every conceivable type of equipment. Forest and hillside, nook and cranny, every spare square mile began to pile high and wide with 'ammo' dumps and vehicle and tank parks, in essence, a fortress bursting at the seams, together with many thousands of U.S. troops, and more arriving daily.

Like my father, who was a brilliant engineer, I was, naturally, mechanically-minded. I was determined that, as I was too young to go to war, I would expend my energies creating my own. I did not realise it then, but I was about to embark on a great adventure. Oh boy! the greatest ever, one that most lads only dream of. I was a fairly tough lad,

Ludgershall Infants' School, 1933: Jim Stoodley, fair hair on right with Ethel Hersey, sitting on his right. (Photo: Courtesy Ethel Hersey)

brought up with a large family, and my parents struggled most of the time to make ends meet in these very difficult times. My early days at school did not give any hint of my devilry to come. There is a jocular saying about Wiltshire lads being all muscle and no brains, but I proved we had ample supplies of both.

The earliest recollection of my first schooldays was about 1933, when I was five years old. It was at the Ludgershall Infants' School and Miss Waters was the teacher. In our class I can only remember a few of my friends. Len Watton, who was to grow up to get married and become a successful businessman in Ludgershall. Ethel Bowman, who also later married and went to live in Andover as Mrs Ethel Hersey. Miss Waters, our teacher, still lives in the village at the time of writing.

I am a great believer in fate, always have been. Probably, I took all those chances from the days of my youth because I believed that nothing could happen to me unless it was meant to be. I always felt I had an extra sense when it came to dealing with danger.

In early years, just before the 1939 war, I trained myself to a high peak of fitness, especially in running. I used to run after hares out on the Downs and run myself to exhaustion time and time again. Each time I could run faster and further – but never caught the hare! Because of this training I was always the best runner at the school sports, and it also got me away, quickly, from a lot of trouble!

Wiltshire was a beautiful county, summer or winter, but especially summer. One could walk for miles through forests crowded with numerous flowers, wild animals and trees of all types, silver birch was in abundance, as was the oak, also yew and beech. The ground was very chalky after you dug down two or three feet and many flints were evident.

The Tidworth Tattoo was, by definition, a spectacle of soldiers marching. I remember the years before the 1939 war as it was a very special occasion to go to the Tattoo, as Tidworth had always been a garrison town. The show was spectacular, with the enemy troops always losing the mock battles that were staged. The advantages of living on Salisbury Plain were many!

I was very mechanically minded, always the very active sort of lad. I loved the country life and I always found sleeping out at night exciting. Salisbury Plain had many old disused army huts and trench systems scattered all over the place and if you looked carefully, you could find a relic from the past!

Many generations of soldiers had trained in this vast area and there were, at one time or other, troop convoys driving about the countryside. Nearly every recruit to the British Army must have, at some time, passed through here on their way to different battlefields, some, no doubt, with good, and bad, memories.

There were a a lot of married quarters at Tidworth, and a lot of army barracks, but only a few private residences. Tidworth House was the most attractive. It was rumoured that the ghost of the little army drummer boy used to haunt the place, and the beating of his drum is supposed to have kept many a resident awake at night!

Perham Down was definitely a 'sneeze and you miss it' place between Ludgershall and Tidworth. A couple of shops and a lot of officers' quarters, which all seemed *la-de-la* to me and, even on a fine day, the outlook from the bloody place was bleak. This part of the world, however, was not meant to be too relaxing, as it was strictly an intensive training area, where some of the best troops in the world were put through their paces.

Most of my leisure hours were spent roaming over this huge area and, if you were not familiar with all the landmarks, you could soon find yourself lost, but I knew my way around, wasn't I born here? While the 'Plain' was, for the most part, barren, there were many large wooded areas, where you could go and really enjoy yourself and some of these stretched for several miles. There was always plenty of wildlife about, despite the noise of gunfire, which never seemed to deter the animals. Yes, this was the place to live if you wanted adventure and fresh air. Mind you, you could get a few stray bullets up you backside if you strayed out on to the rifle ranges, if you were stupid enough to ignore the red flag flying!

The troops used to booze in the Ram Hotel at Tidworth and, to sober up, used to jump into the River Bourne, which was not far from the front door. Others visited the bars in Ludgershall, where they had the choice of three, and, while there were always lots of soldiers around the place, they did not, unduly, upset the village life.

It was now late summer in 1939 and war had been declared. I might see a bit of real action, now that all the men of eligible age were being called up for the various services and, as I was only eleven-and-a-half, I was too young to go and fight the Gerries but, by the looks of things a few months later when it seemed the enemy would try to invade England, I decided that I would do my utmost to resist them if they came anywhere near Wiltshire! Yes, I had decided that I would fight to my last bullet! But, first, I had to prepare . . .

CHAPTER 2

Tidworth Down Senior School

I REMEMBER the siren at Ludgershall being first tested. The eerie wailing sound was an omen of things to come! Not long after we moved up to Tidworth Down Senior, a newly-built school just one mile from Ludgershall, we all got together in the classrooms and, as the new school resembled something of a glass house, we all helped cut strips of bandage, about two inches wide, and glued it in crosses on the large panes on the windows and doors of this two-storied marvel. Hopefully, that would stop them shattering all over us if there was an air attack!

A long brick air-raid shelter, with a solid concrete flat roof, stood out alongside the playground. Not much good for the people inside it if a bomb landed nearby and the heavy roof dropped on them! But Tidworth Down Senior was to be a lucky place, as a bomb never landed within its boundaries. The nearest it came to damage from the air was when I flew over and nearly knocked the flag-pole down some time later!

From the classroom windows the view was fantastic, particularly in the summer. We had the best sports field in the county and I loved sports day because I took part in all the events there and, usually, won the hundred yards and most which involved running or long-jumping.

Our Headmaster, Mr James, was a good 'Head'. Very tall, maybe six foot seven inches. He used to drive his old Daimler daily from his home in Chute. If he drove past you, it looked like he was sitting in the back seat, as his legs were so long. He was fairly strict but, generally speaking, as there was a war on and pressures were on us all, things seemed to run fairly smoothly.

There were, probably, up to four hundred pupils attending the school, mostly from Ludgershall, Tidworth, Shipton Bellinger, Everleigh, Collingbourne and so on, quite a mixture of boys and girls.

I remember the shower at the school, quite a novelty at the time. I used to slip in on the quiet and have a few extra rinses because, at home there was usually a queue waiting to get a bath!

John, my younger brother by one-and-a-half years, and I would go up to Windmill Hill most nights after school, or at weekends. Our latest craze was a trolley we had built with old pram wheels, with a long plank along the length and a large pole tied in the centre carrying a large sail. We called it our land-yacht! As soon as we hoisted the sail up off we went at full belt, providing there was a good breeze in that particular direction, and there usually was on Salisbury Plain! A local farmer, Mr Bridgeman, who owned Sweet Apple Farm, paced us at forty-five miles per hour in his car, which was very fast, considering your behind was only six inches off the ground! The tarmac road went for one mile from east to west

Castledown School (formerly Tidworth Down Senior). Note: Flag-pole Jim near-missed over-flying the school December 1942. (Photo: Courtesy Frank Gamble, 1994)

through the camp and, at the finish of the run, we had to pull the 'land-yacht' back to the other end and start all over again, but this was so exciting and we did not mind at all having the long push back to have another exhilarating trip!

On other days we would go out with out bows and arrows and, at that particular time, there were a lot of sheep killings by a few wild dogs which were roaming the Wiltshire Downs and a local farmer, who had lost a few sheep that way, offered five-shillings (a princely sum) on the production of a wild dog carcass. So, John and I chose one Sunday to

Our land-yacht at Windmill Camp.

hunt over a wide radius and shoot one of these wild dogs with our bows and arrows!

The day was unbearably hot and we walked for miles, keeping close to where sheep were grazing, but as noon approached we had not spotted one wild dog! By 3 p.m. we were beginning to get desperate, and very hungry, as our few meagre sandwiches had long gone and our bottle of water was just a memory! We sat beneath an old, craggy oak tree, not a farthing between us, no food and no prospects!

"Stupid idea of yours, this wild dog hunting, there ain't none anywhere!" says John, kicking the ground with the tip of his boot.

"Be patient, mate," I said.

"Patient!" replied John, "them farmers are just having us on. Anyway, have you got any fags?"

I only had half a Woodbine I found on our way up. I took it, gingerly, out of my fag-tin and, lighting it up, got a safety pin and stuck it through the side and handed it to John for a few puffs! The pin was handy because you could smoke it right down without burning your fingertips, and got more drags!

19

"Come on, John! Hand it over! You've had about five drags on it!"

"No I haven't, you tight-fisted sod!" he replied, handing me the tiny stub. I had one good drag and stamped it well out, as there was always a great danger of fires, particularly in the hot weather.

"Come on, John. Let's have a look for a little longer and then head for home."

"... a bloody dead wild dog!"

We walked another couple of miles and then skirted round the edge of Collingbourne Woods and back towards Crawlboys Farm. It was then that John spotted it in the undergrowth!

"Jim, quick, come here!" he shouted.

"What now?" I replied.

"Quick! A bloody dead wild dog!"

I ran over to where he was pointing and, sure enough, there it was, a wild dog, lying outstretched on its side, looking the part with its jaws open and teeth bared in death. I was staring hard at this five-bob lying on the ground before us and John said: "I'll go and get the farmer and we'll get paid out on the dot!"

"Hang on, John," I cautioned, "it's got to look like we just shot it dead!" I pulled an arrow from my quiver and placed it in the bow and stood back, taking a steady aim. TWANG! the arrow sped to its target at full speed – then bounced off!

"It's bloody hard as iron!" John shouted, "it must have been dead a week!" He took one of his arrows and, with both hands, rammed it into the dead dog!

"He's definitely dead now!" he laughed, "you wait here and I'll get the farmer," and off he went! I sat down close by and started, mentally, to spend my half of the reward! Within half-an-hour John came running back out of breath.

"He's just coming, and if it's a wild dog he'll pay up!" he panted.

After a few minutes, the farmer arrived and glanced down at the dog which, from a few feet, looked as if it had just passed away, then gave us two shiny half-crowns. We put the money in our pockets and it was just then that he bent down and turned the wild dog over with his foot. As he rolled it over, where it had lain there for days, it was all mildewed! We started to walk away, slowly increasing speed, then it dawned on him!

"Hi! You young varmints, come here!" But we were legging up the hill from Crawlboys! There was no way we could part with the half-crowns, and, with the farmer's curses fading in the distance, we headed back to Ludgershall, and home!

CHAPTER 3

The Grand Plan

WINDMILL HILL army camping ground was very large, maybe about four square miles of green turf and, to me, the grass never seemed to grow more than three inches. Here and there, dotted about the site, were various buildings which, when the camp was in use, soldiers would use for washing, toilets and one or two very nice swimming pools. To a young lad, like myself, it was always very exciting, wandering around, especially on the few occasions when the camp was unoccupied, pushing open creaking doors of old store-rooms where, on the odd occasion, I would find an item of army equipment. Sometimes a bandolier, or a few ·303 bullets, maybe the odd rusty bayonet. What great times these were!

Then, there was the time I found an officer's beautiful dress sword. I remember the name engraved near the hilt – 'Eisenhuer". The handle was bound in gold wire, with a highly polished guard. I found this sheathed sword in a wooden foot locker, which was in a shallow hole, buried under dozens of rotten sandbags. Also in the locker was a pair of army boots, a nice pair of brown leather shoes and an officer's cap, still bearing the rather tarnished badge of the Royal Engineers. These, and many other items, added to my collection, made quite a pile under my bed at No.1. South View in Ludgershall.

There seemed to me to be very few Tommies on Salisbury Plain as the war seemed to gobble them up in different parts of the world, where many were dying and others being taken prisoner. As I stood on Windmill Hill on this lovely summer day, my young mind could not understand how one man, namely Adolf Hitler, could bring about so much misery and death to so many innocent people.

Not so far from where I stood, just about a hundred miles away, the German Army was poised to evade England. I was too young to join up, but I had to make serious plans to defend my home and my village, Ludgershall. Time we had little of. I had to get some weapons together, food supplies, in the form of army rations, ammunition, including hand grenades and, of course, one or more machine-guns, with several hiding places at key points around Ludgershall where, if I had to fight the enemy, I could fight a running battle from well-camouflaged positions on high ground. I wondered if any other lads of my age had the same idea as I had, but I knew of no-one who would join me if it came to a shoot-out, except my younger brother, John. He, like myself, was a marksman with a rifle, and not short on guts!

I, with John, had plenty of target practice out on the firing ranges at the back of Tidworth with the Short Lee Enfield rifle, about ten pounds in weight. This rifle was highly accurate in expert hands. One could maintain a high rate of fire with a nine-round magazine, easy to keep clean and not heavy to carry, even for a youngster like myself.

I had joined the local Home Guard Cadets and had learned a lot in training exercises but, if, and when, the Germans invaded, I calculated that, as Wiltshire lay about thirty miles inland, enemy airborne troops would certainly try to establish strong-points in our area, if this happened, I certainly would not report to my local drill hall, where I would come under the command of persons who, in my opinion, did not have the same strategy in mind as I had, so I would make my own way to my first defence position, uncover my weapons and fight and kill any enemy troops who approached. My plan was always to fight and slowly withdraw to pre-planned, and well-stocked, defences. I vowed to have a great stock of machine-gun ammunition, and guns, at each point. Fighting the enemy and killing as many as I could would be easy, I thought. Staying alive would be the big problem, so surprise would have to be my aim at all times and, if I died defending my part of the country, then so be it, many others had already done so! I didn't want to die, so if I could live through all this and be around the day we won the war, that would be worth all the effort.

I was sorry I was not older because then I would not have to get arms and equipment by devious means (stealing is the right word) but, in my mind, it was a means to an end. Any day, in the near future, we could all find ourselves surrounded by a lot of big blond bastards. I just could not imagine them charging through our village, killing whoever stood against them, but it was a real possibility, and almost a certainty, so I planned to be ready and fight my war my way but, under all the circumstances, my plans must remain 'private'.

I used to sit up late at night by my bedroom window, with my Lee Enfield resting on the window-ledge behind the cover of curtains and would draw a bead on an unsuspecting passerby, pretending to aim a shot, as if it was a newly-arrived German paratrooper. I could see the searchlights on the horizon, waving to the left and right. This gave me some comfort, as I felt there were others, like me, watching and waiting for those who might think they could just drop in and occupy our country, as easy as Poland and the best part of Europe!

CHAPTER 4

Waltzing Matilda

L OCAL gossip had it that the Aussies were coming to Windmill Hill soon, despite 'the walls have ears' campaign, rumours always seemed to have an element of truth.

What were these so-called 'Aussies' going to be like, I pondered. I looked up Australia on my atlas. Certainly one heck of a long way away, I thought!

Sure enough, within a fortnight, thousands of Australians, in several troop trains, came crowding the sidings at Ludgershall and, for several days, we (John and myself) and several of our friends, had a great time going among the troops, cadging money and cigarettes and just about anything we could lever from them! The whole place seemed awash with khaki and what a noisy, and friendly, lot they were. They eventually arrived at Windmill Camp and, soon, hundreds of tents, bell and marquees, dotted the hillside down to Ludgershall.

Now, if you are hungry and want to get good wholesome grub down you, an army camp is the place to be. At meal-times the usual drill is to go into a soldiers' canteen, get in the meal queue, chat with the troops as you get nearer the serving tables, and put a solemn, hungry look on your face, then when your turn came hold your tin out, hopefully. It always worked for me!

The Aussies were generous to a fault. One corporal gave me a tunic and riding breeches. The breeches I gave to John, together with a pair of putties, which would help keep out the cold in the coming months.

What amazed me most were the big chunks of butter the men were served up. We, in rationed England, were allocated just two ounces a week each! When I told the cookhouse sergeant this, he could not believe it and, promptly, reached down, got hold of two empty sandbags and put a dozen freshly-baked loaves in one and about ten pounds of butter in the other.

"Here, Sport," he mumbled, "take these home to your mum. Just a minute, put these in too!" he added, and passed me two seven-pound tins of corned beef!

"Thanks very much, mate," I replied, "it's very kind of you and Mum will be over the moon!"

"That's okay, son," he replied, "on your way now!" So I hauled the sacks up on my shoulder and trudged off home, so pleased, and impatient to see Mum's face light up when I tipped my load on her kitchen table.

Unfortunately, these kind Aussies did not stay long at Windmill Hill and, within a few weeks, they suddenly departed. Who knows where they eventually sailed to, and how many never returned to their homes will never truly be known.

I felt sad about all this, as no sooner had I made a few new friends then I would wake up one morning, visit the camp, only to find it deserted, not a soul in sight! It seemed that they had been spirited away! All very uncanny to a young, enquiring mind, like mine!

One thing, in particular, I noticed about the Aussies was that they could drink an enormous amount of beer! Where they put it all beats me! They must have had hollow legs!

I left school a year early because of the war crisis, to do my part in the war effort. So far, I had little to fight the Germans with, but events in the very near future were soon to change that situation!

CHAPTER 5

Tim—ber

I WAS still thirteen years old when I finally left Tidworth Down Senior School on Perham Down. The Forestry Commission were taking on many extra workers, of all ages, to work in Collingbourne Woods, a mile or so from Ludgershall, helping to cut down trees and sawing logs up, mainly to be burned in the large charcoal burners situated on the side of the Biddesden – Chute Road. Specialists from Norway, elderly men, set up the kilns with thousands of small logs, laid and stacked inside these large round slow-burners and, after a few days, they would shovel out all the remaining charcoal, bag it up and it would be sent away by the ton-load to the munition factories.

I was given various jobs in the forest. I remember the big Irish foreman coming up to me on my first day, saying "So you're Jimmy Stoodley, eh? Ever used one of these?" and he handed me a large axe. "Here, get hold of this and plough your way through that bloody lot!" pointing to a nearby clump of silver birch, "and don't chop your leg off! Now, sod off!"

I took the axe from him and shuffled off towards my first job in the war effort. The miserable bugger, I thought, I must remember to drop a tree on his head, that'll bring him down to earth, big Irish git, so he is. As I started hacking away at my first 'victim' a lovely-looking Land Army girl walking up behind me and said "Hello, you're Jim Stoodley aren't you?"

I swung round in surprise and nearly sliced her head off!

"Yeah, that's me and who might you be then?"

"I'm Iris, I live up the far side of the woods with my Mum, Dad and sister Alma. I'm seventeen today!"

"Oh, happy birthday then!" I replied, putting down the axe to take a breather. "Yes, this is my first day here. How long have you been a Land Girl then?"

"Only a few months," Iris replied. I was eyeing her up and down while she was chattering away. Not a bad bit of stuff, I thought, even though she looked a little bit tubby in her corduroy breeches.

"Well, Iris," I interrupted, "I must get on and cut a few trees down. I'll see you again, no doubt!"

"Oh, yes, of course," she said, "I must get on with it too. I'll see you again, Jim. Cheerio!" and with that she walked away into the dense forest.

I went back to swinging the axe again. Christ! I thought, there must be an easier way of earning a living! Sweat was running down my back, but what the heck, I'll get used to it after a few days!

The days turned into weeks and, meanwhile, the war situation still remained grave. I got to like my job as a lumberjack but, as I was usually working alone for hours on end, I longed for a job where I felt I was doing a more direct contribution to the war effort.

Meanwhile, I got on to other jobs in the woods, driving the Caterpillar tractor, hauling in some of the larger tree-trunks, which were being cut for the new sawmills springing up.

Soon there were Italian PoWs sent down under guard to help out with the volume of work which was building up. It was then that the food situation at meal breaks improved, as the PoWs were issued with British Army rations, and I made sure I got a few bully-beef sandwiches from the prisoners who could not eat the stuff!

I found, by and large, that the Italian soldiers were easy-going and always ready for a laugh, though a few of them did not appreciate me calling them 'Wogs'. Many of them could speak good English and told me about their families back in Italy. I could not help but feel a little sorry for them but we were at war with Italy still, and our troops were getting killed and wounded, so I made sure that my relationship with them was kept at arm's length.

One morning, when they arrived at the sawmills in the army lorry, they were jumping down from the back and, as the guard in his turn jumped down from the tailboard, he handed his rifle to one of the PoWs to hold for him. He could have easily shot the guard, and several of us too, if he had wanted to, but he casually handed it back when the guard asked him for it. I told the guard that he was stupid giving his rifle to a PoW.

"Don't worry, son, they're on our side now!"

"Look here, mate," I replied, "if you do that again, I'll report you to your CO, so let's have no more of that nonsense!"

"Oh, you just worry too much," he replied.

"Yeah, I do, especially if I happen to get a Lee Enfield stuck against my ribs, and it's obvious you joined the Army Catering Corps straight from the NAAFI!"

"Oh, you're a smart-arse, aren't you?" he retorted.

"No, I just don't want some 'Iti' to put a bullet up it!" I replied and walked away!

It was while I was working here that I had the pleasure to meet Derek

Hill, a young man in his twenties. He used to paint, occasionally, in the woods, as well as working on local farms. He was a friend of my brother Bob, and Derek Hill was very attracted to my sister, Phyllis, and once told her that he would marry her one day, but never did.

I arrived home one evening, really fed up and tired out. Dad had just come in and it was then he told me I would be working soon at Tidworth Depot, doing a real job of work. I wondered what new adventures that job might bring!

Also, that was the day the Japanese attacked the U.S. Naval Base on the Hawaiian Islands, which brought America into the war on our side, to fight the Germans too!

My mind was in a whirl. Did this mean that the U.S. Forces would come to England and to Salisbury Plain? Anyhow, as Dad told me, I would shortly be changing jobs and, who knows, with luck I might meet the Yanks!

CHAPTER 6

The Yanks Are Coming!

ICLEARLY remember the first American troop train steaming down the track from Andover to Ludgershall Station. I was standing in the front garden of our home at 1 South View. The train was tooting its whistle as it slid slowly by. Across the other side of the road, only a few yards from where I was standing, men in strange olive-coloured uniforms were crowded at the carriage windows, waving. I imagined they were all waving just at me and I was shouting "Hello, Yankee Doodle Dandy" which made them all laughed.

I ran across the road with John and a few friends, down the street to the level crossing at Mr Berry's farmyard. Now I was only a few feet from them and out of the carriage windows they were throwing strange packages to us. Most were 'candies', as they called them, we found out, and chewing-gum, also some fags. I liked the Lucky Strike brand best because, I suppose, it had on the packet 'they're toasted'. I never found out what that really meant.

I ran down the railway line alongside the track a few yards to the station. The troop-train was packed solid. There is really something exhilarating about a troop-train, full of troops from a distant country! Just think of all the new friends one could make, especially as they had a lot of of swag to hand out! I felt so happy at the prospect of so many goodies!

We ran up the slope that led on to the long platform (specially designed for long troop-trains) and the special constables shouted to us to get out of the station, so we had to settle for a perch on the station gates, and I peered, anxious up and down the line of carriages, weighing up the pros and cons!

The troops were soon disembarking onto the platform and forming up into rough lines, like a sea of khaki! Then, at the end, I spotted the band forming up! Strange orders were being shouted up and down the lines and soon the band struck up a tune and moved out towards the station gates. Lots of people from the village were lined up on the streets outside and soon the long line of soldiers filed off the station and down the hill. Lots of the local girls were also there, trying to attract the GIs and blowing kisses!

I ran out ahead of the band and marched, proudly, in front, chin up and chest out, swinging my arms. I kept looking round to see if I was in step with them but, strangely it seemed to me, they were out of step with each other!

When I turned right at the Triangle, thinking they were going round and up to Windmill Hill, they went straight up towards Perham Down, and I was left marching on my own, going the wrong way! I felt a fool, as all my mates laughed at me. I ran back to the front again and, proudly took my place. I knew, now, where they were heading and as the band played *The Yanks are Coming* it sent my hair tingling with excitement! I knew, from that moment on, that my life would be influenced, intensely, by the arrival of the American army! Oh, how proud I felt, leading this great column of fighting men, in front of everyone, my heart was pounding with joy. Yes, the Yanks were certainly coming!

When we arrived at Perham Down, I stood back on the side of the road and, as they passed by in long columns, I shouted greetings to them and the more I shouted, the greater the amount of goodies were forthcoming! I'll keep in with these blokes, I thought!

I ran up alongside the marching GIs, joking with them. They were asking "How old's your sister, buddy?"

"Having you got any foreign coins, mate?" I shouted back. In reply, I was overwhelmed with all kinds of different money, cents, dollar bills, quarters and so on! These chaps speak my language, I thought, as I stuffed it all in my pockets. I was loaded, my pockets bulged with American coins, lighters, etc.

"Where d'ya come from, mate?" I shouted to one.

"Wyoming!"

"Arizona!" shouted another.

"Christ, they're all bloody cowboys in disguise, I thought, no wonder they walk funny!

"What's this place called, buddy?" said one.

"Ludgershall," I beamed back at him.

"Big deal!" he replied, laughing.

"Take no notice of him," another shouted, "he's a bum from the Bronx!" A bum, I thought, I've never heard of that expression before, but he did seem to have rather a big arse, as he waddled along the road! The column suddenly halted outside their new campsite and, for a moment, they fell out and sat down on the grass.

"Let's see your rifle, mate," I said to one of the GIs, "I'll show you how the Grenadier Guards slope arms!" A crowd soon gathered around me as I showed them a few of my Army Cadet Force drills.

"You sure are smart with that rifle, buddy!" said a sergeant.

"Yes, I have had to learn to handle it properly, as the Gerries could drop in any time!"

"What's Gerries? Piss pots ain't they?" said a little fellow, picking his nose, and with a tin hat on his head which looked like one!

"Course they ain't, it means Germans, that's what! I shot one Gerry paratrooper two weeks ago, who landed in the cornfield over there!" I lied, pointing behind them. They all turned round, instinctively, mouths wide open!

"Yeah, yeah, I know," laughed the nose-picker, "I guess you minced him up into a German frankfurter too! Right?"

"No," I replied, "I pushed one of his fingers up his nose like you do and I shoved the other up his arse and made him goose-step to the police station!" That made them all burst out laughing and the nose-picker shut up, red-faced.

"You're all right, Jim," shouted one GI, "stick around some, you almost speak our language!"

That was my cue, and I stuck around for quite some time to come but, before I left to go back home, I told them we had no grub in the house, and that my Mum had to take in washing to buy food, (my usual tale) and that brought a cascade of K-rations and all sorts of chocolate, from all directions, with which, I made my way home, shouting my thanks and promising myself I would return to this font of overflowing kindness at the crack of dawn, with a bloody great sack!

I trudged back home, carrying all my loot. Charlie Hawkins had also had a field-day further down the line of troops.

"Done well today, Jim," he shouted.

"Yeah, we sure have, Charlie!" We were just not able to believe our luck!

CHAPTER 7

The Plan

I HAD just started working on my new job in the Depot, which was the large REME ordnance repair complex in Tidworth, employed as an apprentice fitter. I was sent down to the Tank Shop, which was a giant building, where one could see dozens of tanks and other armoured vehicles in various stages of repair. I spent a few weeks at different departments and, eventually, settled for the tank preparation unit. Now, this place was just right for learning the ropes, as I had a good instructor by the name of Sergeant Single of the U.S. Army, and I managed to learn a lot about the Sherman tank and its weapon!

I soon got into a few scrapes and one day nearly electrocuted the electrician foreman, so, eventually, I was transferred to the Motor Pool, where my Dad was in charge. My job was to service the vehicles there, some makes being GMC, Studebaker, Mac and Jeeps. I drove them all, unofficially, and soon became a fairly good driver.

On my time off I was building my own aeroplane. I had plans, and needed a plane to fulfil them! A land-owner, then Mrs Elisabeth Bryan Guinness, lent me what was then known to me as the Long field at the bottom of Crawlboys. I think she obliged just to get rid of me! I was looked on, locally, as a bit of a head-case, so I suppose there was a general feeling that I may just fly away for good and leave them in peace!

Lots of people would come and watch me at weekends working on my plane as it, slowly, took some kind of resemblance to the 'Flying Flea'.

"There's definitely something wrong with him!" I would hear some mutter, as they looked on. There were also remarks such as: "Do you want an elastic band, Jimmy?" or, "Forget your parachute, won't you!" but it only made me more determined to finish it. The local detective would also call down and, casually, drop hints like: "You know you have got to have a licence lad?" and things like that!

"Oh, don't worry," I replied, "I won't take off till I have one!" Smarmy sod he was, and as he walked off he received a few rude gestures!

I was tuning up an old Austin Seven engine to fit in the plane and I was waiting for a set of piston rings, and one or two other bits, so it seemed that it wouldn't be too long before I could start her up!

I returned home from work a few weeks later and, after having my tea,

I went down to Crawlboys to the long field and, as I drew near, I could see the smoke and flames that, only a short time ago, was my pride and joy. Who could have done this? I found out, later, that my Mum and sister, Phyllis, had gone down in the afternoon and set fire to my plane, afraid that I would take off and kill myself (much to the disappointment of some of the locals!) I could not believe it! All those hours I had spent there, and now all there was to show for my efforts was just a pile of ashes! Women! They had no sense of adventure, I thought. Now the shit had really hit the fan!

The war was going badly for us, and for me too! I wanted to get into the war properly and have a go at those bloody Germans, but how? Then one day I thought I had the answer. I had hit on this brainwave. Now, if I could get to Germany, and being a lad I could move around easier without being too noticeable, I may be able to get to Berlin and assassinate that bloody Hitler! Yes, that could work, with a lot of luck. They wouldn't suspect a lad of my age trying this and, after all, I was blond, had a big square head, and could play dumb and travel mostly at night. All I needed was a small plane really! Perhaps I could pinch one off the Yanks, fly it to the Long field and hide it up for a few days, until I sorted out my stores for the trip!

Now, I could get hold of a few hand-grenades, some sub-machine guns etc., I would also need a few cans of spare fuel. This was easy to come by. All I needed was a lot of nerve and luck! I would get as far as I could by air. crossing the Channel to France and, when all my fuel was used up, I could land in some remote spot, burn the aircraft, and lay low for a while, then make my way to Berlin. Meanwhile, the Fuhrer would remain oblivious of my planned assault on his Third Reich! If I wore my Home Guard Cadet uniform and was captured, I would be treated as a prisoner of war, but I didn't intend to get caught! Still, always best to be on the safe side! If I did manage to pull this off, think of the headlines in the papers: 'Boy of fourteen machine-guns Herr Hitler to death' or 'Jim Stoodley receives the Victoria Cross'. All these pictures flashed through my mind!

I then remembered the polo field near Perham Down. The US Army had an airstrip there, in fact it was the largest and the first of its type in England. There were about ten Piper Cub light aircraft there, which they used for spotting the artillery, and for ferrying officers about. Here is my chance, I thought! But the best laid plans have their problems and this one was no different, and one big problem here was that I did not think the U.S. Army would take too kindly to someone stealing one of their aeroplanes! The Yanks had a reputation for shooting first and asking questions later! Trigger-happy buggers they were! One more small detail was that I had never flown before, but, if I could get off the ground I would learn soon enough!

Now, the next step was to pinch a plane when they were looking the other way, which was fairly frequently!

John, my younger brother, was thirteen years old, a tough lad, and always ready for a lark, but when I told him that I planned to fly off to kill Hitler he said, "You must be out of your bloody mind!" However, when I explained that I only wanted him to help me to pinch the plane and take it to the Long field where I would drop him off, he changed his mind and agreed to come along for just a short ride!

Early the next Sunday, we went up to the polo field for a reconnoitre. On one side of the airstrip was a wood which was very convenient for sneaking up unobserved, and to make our plans!

As we crept out of the woods we could see about ten of these aircraft neatly lined up on our side, tied down and covered up with canvas sheeting. What a sight for sore eyes, I thought, all I need to do is to pick the one with the most fuel. I looked down to the other end of the airstrip, and there was my first surprise, a light tank! It had a 37mm gun and a ·30-calibre machine-gun mounted on the turret!

"Christ, that's all I need!" I said to John.

Looking closer, I could make out a sentry, smoking, with his head just visible out of the top of the turret, but not showing any interest our way, and, after a while, he disappeared down inside the tank.

"Right, John, now's our chance. I'll go and have a look at the planes and see if there is anything suitable!" So saying, I put my head down and crept along to the far end of the line of aircraft and opened the door of a plane which had a stencilled name on its nose, *Shirley Anne*, which was next to a plane called *Sad Sack*. I climbed into the front cockpit and sat in the seat. This was a great feeling! I wondered if there was an instruction book, but could not see one.

I glanced round the cockpit, noting all the dials. Above my head were two switches for left and right magneto, then the airspeed indicator, artificial horizon, and so on. I rested my feet on the rudder pedals and tried them, left and right, took the joystick in my hands and watched the left and right aileron tilt up and down as I moved it side to side. The Ki-gas pump was very much the same as in the Sherman tanks which I was very familiar with and had driven. The Shermans were fitted with an aircraft nine-cylinder radial engine (on early models) and also were fitted with left and right magneto control switches so, basically, I could cope with the starting procedures, but I did not fancy swinging that propeller to start her up. Nevertheless, take off I would, and fly, but not yet! I would need to plan things out in detail a little more!

I crept back the way I had come and joined John, who was shivering in the cold, waiting for me. I had found half a pack of Lucky Strike 'fags' in the plane and we enjoyed a smoke.

"Well," said John, taking a puff from his cigarette, "what do you think, Jim?"

"Let's bugger-off," I replied and "and think it over!"

We returned home and, over the next few days, I spent many hours deep in thought, sifting my mind over and over. The longer I thought about it, the more I began to doubt my ability. Why did I have to fly the damned thing? Well, I thought, here is a heaven-sent opportunity and I couldn't let it pass me by. I had to make up my mind. I had to pick a day, like a Sunday when, perhaps, there might be a more relaxed attitude on security. Would the weather be favourable? It all depended on a lot of things all being right at once. Aside from that, a very chancy thing indeed, and the Yanks weren't going to take this lying down. Also, there was the tank parked at the end of the airfield, which did not overfill me with optimism!

John was to accompany me to the airfield on the day and help me uncover and wheel the plane out into the starting position. What I did not know was that the plane we would eventually steal had been used, personally, by the Major in charge of the field, and on the nose of that plane was stencilled, boldly, his wife's *Shirley Anne*. I would have good cause to remember that name to this day, forty years on!

CHAPTER 8

Sneak Attack

D AD told me to creosote the double gate as he backed his car out of the garden on to Central Street. I had been dodging this job for some time and he was getting impatient with me.

"Make sure you get on with it now. The creosote and brush are in the garage, and don't get it all over the pavement! he shouted, as he drove off down the hill on his way to Andover.

Today was Saturday, and just after breakfast, so I had plenty of time to get it done and have some time to go off and see some pals of mine along Short Street. I went back into the house. Mum was in the kitchen doing the washing up in the large, old, stone sink. There always seemed to be an endless pile of crockery forthcoming from the kitchen table where my nine brothers and four sisters took turns to sit down. Mind you, we all took turns at the sink, but Mum always seemed to be there.

"Dad's just told me to do the big gate, Mum."

"What's wrong with it, Jim?"

"Oh, nothing, just wants me to put a coat of creosote on."

"Oh," she replied, "well don't come in here after, washing your hands in my sink, stinking it out with paint, will you?"

"O.K. Mum."

I looked up at the old clock on the mantelpiece, which showed 10 a.m. The weather was dry, with low clouds, so I put my old army coat on and went out and collected the brush and creosote from the garage.

As I started brushing away at the gate, humming to myself, Harvey Perry came down Central Street and stopped for a chat. Harvey was about the same age as me, and lived up at the far end of Short Street, in fact his house was at the end of a long row, so if you weren't careful, on a dark night you could step out of the back door and walk right onto the ploughed field, which came up to the back door. Occasionally, 'Harv' would come on a few rides with me when I borrowed a jeep or truck from the Yanks, and we would go for a trip around Chute, or somewhere quiet, away from the roving Army MPs.

"Hello, Jim," he said, squatting on the nearby fence.

"Hello, Harv, where ya going, mate?"

"Only down to Workman's shop to get a few things for me mum."

"Oh yeah," I replied, "you going to the Garrison Theatre tonight? There's a good film on."

"Is there, Jim, what's it called?"

"*Gone With the Wind*, Harv."

"Okay, Jim, I'll see you tonight at the pictures. Right?"

"Yes, about seven, Harv."

"Okay, Jim" said Harv, and off he went to the shops.

Oh well, I thought, better get on with this bloody job, so I carried on brushing away. Soon, I was conscious of the sound of distant aeroplane engines, which seemed to die away after a few minutes. I didn't like the sound of them. Sounded very much like Gerries, I'd heard them often enough before! Shortly after, the air-raid sirens sounded and I thought I'd better go inside and make sure Mum gets down to our air-raid shelter near the back door. As I went in through the back door Mum was doing the ironing on a sheet on the kitchen table, quite unconcerned!

"Come on, Mum, get down the shelter, there's a raid on!"

"They're not chasing me down a shelter, them Gerries, I've got all this ironing to finish!"

"All right, Mum, but if they come close you'll have to come down."

I ran outside and stood by the gate, searching the clouds. I could hear the planes again but couldn't see any yet. People were hurrying home from all directions, but I stood my ground, still searching the sky, when I saw a bomber sneak, briefly, out of the clouds and then back in! I looked right up Central Street to the top of the hill and it was then I saw them! Two black bombers, one behind the other, in a straight line, and they were only a few hundred feet above the ground, flying straight towards me! It was too late, it seemed, for me to run, so I just stood rooted to the ground right out in full view of the Gerries.

They came roaring towards me, the thunder of their twin motors echoing between the houses on either side of Central Street, and as the first plane flew over my head I could see the man in the nose of the plane peering down at me! Then, with a 'woosh' he was gone towards Perham Down. Then number two came up and over my head, following his leader, and soon after I could near the explosions of their bombs dropping on the camp at Perham.

I ran in to get Mum down to the shelter, and there she was, still ironing! I dragged her by the hand out to the shelter.

"Come on, Mum, a joke's a joke!"

"All-right," she replied, as she, reluctantly, came below ground.

"Here, sit here, Mum. No-one else in the house, is there?"

"No, they're all out. I hope they have the sense to keep inside till the raid's over."

"Yes, so do I," I replied.

After about fifteen minutes, the all-clear signal sounded, so we clambered out of the shelter and stood in the garden. Many people had started to gather by their garden gates and were talking about the air-raid. Mrs Wilde came walking down to where we stood together with her son Eddie and gave Mum her version, in colourful terms, about what she would do if she got her hands on the German pilots. "I'd castrate the buggers," she was telling Mum and was indicating that none of them had any fathers!

I made my way back to the gate I was working on and continued to brush on the creosote. Tom Humphries, who was about my age and lived opposite, came over to ask me if I had seen the planes. I replied that I had, and that they passed overhead.

"They didn't, did they, Jim?" Tom exclaimed, looking surprised.

"Yes, I could see the gunner in the nose and I threw a stone up at them and they opened up on me, but I dodged behind the gate-post and the bullets went just by me!"

Tom didn't know whether I was spinning him a yarn, but, as he had been inside the house, he had to give me the benefit of the doubt!

"Me and Harvey are going to the pictures tonight, Tom," I said, "want to come with us?"

"Okay, yes, I will, Jim. I've got a tanner, so that will be enough, won't it?"

"Not if you're treating me as well, Tom!" I laughed, as he went back into his garden.

We all met up that evening at the cinema at Tidworth and had to wait in the long queue outside. There were crowds of U.S. Army soldiers and their girlfriends waiting to see *Gone With the Wind*. Harvey didn't have enough money to get in, so I hit on an idea to raise a few pennies.

"Look, Harv, you play your mouth-organ and we will walk slowly up and down the queue and I'll sing a couple of songs!"

"O.K. Jim, that's a good idea!" So off we set, slowly walking down the queue, with me belting out *When Irish Eyes are Smiling*. There couldn't have been many Irish descendants in the queue, because by the time we got to the end we had the princely sum of threepence. We were looking at the paltry collection when the manager walked up to us and shouted "Clear off, you little sods, no beggars allowed here! Go on, clear off!" Harvey was pretty big for his age and wasn't going to be done out of his

39

entrance fee, so told the manager to bugger off or else the three of us would give him a hiding!

"Yeah? just you try," he replied and then started to push Harvey away from the queue.

A couple of Yanks, seeing we were getting pushed around, told the manager to knock if off, saying "Leave the guys alone, buddy, you're twice their size!" With that, the manager smartly disappeared into the crowd!

"Here, you guys," one of the Yanks called out, "go ahead and play *Yankee Doodle Dandy,*" and with that, threw down a couple of coins. Harvey, who was trying to belt out the tune and didn't know it properly, just kept playing, regardless! Soon, many of the GIs were throwing halfpennies, pennies, shillings and all sorts of coins. We scrambled to collect them off the ground and soon the queue started to move as the doors opened. We counted the collection, which altogether amounted to fifteen shillings or so. That meant five-bob each, a small fortune to young lads such as ourselves, and there would be plenty of cash to spare for fags and sweets!

We decided to go up into the expensive seats in the balcony where all the toffs sat, at two-shillings a seat.

When the film was over we all filed out into the blackout and made our way to the bus stop at Hampshire Cross and were soon back in Ludgershall.

Harvey and Tom said goodnight and I made my way home after what was a very profitable evening! Tomorrow would be a new day, and more excitement! Who would know! We were just living from one day to the next and as more American troops were arriving with their masses of equipment, things looked a little better for us!

CHAPTER 9

Twenty Sub-Machine Guns

ONE lovely Sunday morning, John and I decided to go for a walk out over the downs. It was seven in the morning and we wanted to creep out before the rest of the family were up and about. We set off, past the Triangle, walking on, innocently, past the little Police Station, then over Windmill Hill, towards the vast Downs which lay before us.

Today was a special time for us, as I wanted to collect a few machine-guns and a good supply of 'ammo' and out there, beyond us, the whole countryside was stockpiled with every conceivable kind of weapon one could name, but well concealed from view!

What I specifically required was a light machine-gun and a lot of ammo, as there was a good market for rabbit meat and hares. There were thousands of rabbits on Salisbury Plain at this time and many hares, in fact, the rabbit warrens which crowded each and every hillside were the homes for just hundreds at a time. Now, rabbits scare easily, and to creep up over open ground on them, unseen, takes a lot of camouflage, patience and skill. Furthermore, once a shot was fired, the rabbits feeding above ground close to their burrows would bolt down their holes! I reasoned that both of us, firing machine-guns on a spray arc of fire, could knock off quite a few at each go! At this rate we should make a lot of 'dough' and, just think, we could afford to pay two shillings at the Garrison Theatre picture house up in the balcony and even take my girlfriend too! Yes, shooting and selling these rabbits certainly had a bright future but, first let's get the guns!

The sun was getting warmer as we walked on and on. We were getting close to a vast wooded area, where I knew there were all kinds of U.S. army equipment hidden from view, and covered with camouflage netting.

"Come on, John, let's clear the nets and read what it says on the boxes!"

"No!" said John, "I want to have something to eat first!" and he opened his back-pack, taking out some broken biscuits.

"Wait!" I said, trying to make out the stencilling on the boxes in front of me. Gradually, it dawned on me. There it was, plain as day – K and C Rations – on each large waterproofed box! There must have been at least one hundred boxes, each box holding, maybe, fifty one-man rations! God!

Enough to feed us for five years, I thought, and -crash, bang, I smashed one case open!

John sat there with his mouth wide open, then he was on his feet beside me, scrambling for a box! He always carried a sheath-knife and he ripped the wax-covered brown paper off the packets and "Gosh, just look look at that!" he shouted. First there was a pack of five Chesterfield fags, then small tins of meat, a lot of malt and glucose tablets, coffee, powdered milk, sugar and so on. Boy! What a feast!

We must have gone through about four K rations and then decided to cover the rest, carefully, back up again. This was a great discovery, as we could later collect a good supply and hide them, but we still had to find the guns!

We moved on to other piles of supplies. Artillery, shells, rifle bullets. On to others, bazookas all crated up, mortar barrels and bombs, hand-grenades, and on the list went, until – ah! here we are at last! There before us was another huge pile of crates marked 'sub-machine guns'! We opened the first case and inside there they were, all in separate complete packs, all greased up! It is surprising how small a box a machine-gun will pack into, and I reckoned there were twenty guns in each case, packed separately. John and I carried the heavy case back down the hill. Not a soul was in sight. Good! This was a hot day, but we must get at least another mile to the next wood!

There were a lot of fir tree plantations in the area, some about half a mile long by half as wide, about ten feet high, and very dense. They were ideal for hiding out in, and we decided to dig a dug-out just inside the edge of one of these and make a 'headquarters' here, to stockpile K-rations and all our weapons!

We spent several odd days fitting out our hideout, making it very comfy and waterproof and, most important, absolutely invisible from outside. Then we had to go back and search for point-forty-five bullets for the machine-guns and soon had a reserve of about five thousand rounds. I also added my Dad's Home Guard Lee Enfield rifle, as he never used it and never missed it! All in all, we had a large supply of everything we needed, particularly American fags, blankets and magazines of ammo!

On most weekends we slept out in our hideout, cooking on a little primus stove. Occasionally, the odd U.S. soldiers would drive close by in tanks or jeeps, but we were never discovered at that time.

It would soon be time to go out and test the machine-guns with John but, first, I would have to assemble them, washing off all the protective grease. Eventually, I got the job completed and we set the day!

United States of America
M3A1

The M3A1's utilitarian appearance reflects the fact that it was designed for ease in mass-production. It won its nickname, "grease gun", because of its strong resemblance to that piece of equipment.

45" ACP

The Grease Gun.

The sub-machine guns had a magazine which also served as a hand grip. It held twenty-nine rounds of ·45 'ammo', at least that's all I managed to get in the 'mag' and we both carried about six spare magazines. It had a metal extendible shoulder stock and a pistol grip like a revolver. I could fire a single shot with a quick trigger finger. It was also a very lightweight gun, popular with all GIs, they nicknamed it the 'Greasegun'. It was also my favourite. You could not call it accurate, but on rapid fire, and at close range, you couldn't miss! Just spray the bullets like a hosepipe!

One day we found a half-track armoured vehicle and, as no-one was about, we pinched the fifty-calibre machine-gun off its mounting! Boy, was that heavy! Later, I eventually got a proper tripod mounting from the 'dump' and, now, our hideout sported a ·50 machine gun! I used to scan the sky some days, waiting for the Gerries to come over low, but they must have been tipped off by the local spies and, up to now, I never had the pleasure.

The fifty-calibre was very heavy. It took two of us to lift it up on the tripod mounting, so I decided to leave it mounted and cover it with its special sheath zipped cover.

In our spare time we used to clean all our weapons and make sure the ammo was kept dry and in a cool place. I had made up my mind that if the German paratroopers landed near us we could hold out for a long time. We had large stocks of food, ammunition, weapons and now we were filling sandbags to make a wall, two feet high, around our hideout, and covering them with fir-tree branches, from five yards we were invisible! We always made sure we showed no light at night. Yes, we were ready for anything at any time!

I was short of cash and I thought it was time to try and get some rabbits. I heard, on the grapevine, that their fetching price was up to five shillings each, that was, of course, if you could shoot them, and not blow them into bits, although it was difficult with a machine-gun not to do that!

We set out after tea, as sunset was the favourite feeding time for the rabbits. We had to allow an hour or so to crawl up, undetected, on the rabbit warren, which was on the side of an exposed hillside. John was about ten yards one side of me and, together, we painfully edged closer, waited until we were fifty yards away, then at a nod we would open fire together. We sprayed bullets from left to right, the rabbits raced to get to the safety of their holes. Legs, heads, tails, went flying in all directions and, when the magazines were empty, we would run out and collect the bits and the odd complete rabbit! Our best score was eleven for fifty-odd rounds of ammo, and I would put them in a supply parachute canopy and, after dark, deliver them to eager customers, who were not particular if they were in bits or not!

As there were several firing ranges all over this area of the Downs, the sound of firing guns went, mostly, unnoticed.

Cleaning the weapons took a lot of time and safety precautions had to be observed, as you could easily shoot someone accidentally, ourselves included. The barrel of the 'greasegun' unscrewed easily so in that respect it was easier to clean than the other larger weapons. The bullets on the fifty-calibre were very heavy and one belt took some lifting from its box on to the feed side of the gun. It took both hands to pull back the bolt on this gun, which had a large handle on it, and I liked the two fist grips with the trigger in between them, very easily pressed by either thumb. It might shake the life out of me if I fired it! I longed for a German aircraft to fly over, or a load of enemy paratroopers coming down around me, I felt I could win the whole bloody war on my own with that fifty-calibre! I wanted to cock the gun and have a go, but there were some tracer bullets mixed in the belt, and I did not want to give the position of our hideout away, as it was the most important to keep that absolutely secret between John and myself.

As the days went by, our arsenal grew! I had to build my own little caches, all within handy reach, just in case we were attacked. I made sure that, whatever else happened, I would not run out of ammo or food, unlike the movies we saw when the U.S. Army nearly always ran short of something or other, when fighting the Indians. No, Sir! We weren't going to be caught in that predicament! I just hoped that the Gerries didn't find out about my defences, or they may bypass me if they landed and I would lose my chance to have a go at them!

CHAPTER 10

We Take Off On Sunday

AFTER a few days of further planning, I decided that, barring unseen circumstances, like bad weather, getting shot, etc., I would take off on Sunday morning at about 11 a.m. on the 13th December, 1942, and my flight-plan would be: to the McDougall's Flour Mills tower on the edge of Andover, Hampshire, next to the railway station five air miles from the take-off point, then make a part turn, follow the railway-line back past Weyhill and on back to Ludgershall. As our house, 1 South View, was alongside the railway I would see it easily. I would, then, follow the railway up over Collingbourne Ducis, continue on to Savernake Tunnel and turn right about and retrace my course via the railway again, and have another look over Ludgershall. From there, I would head out, this time following the main road to Everleigh, then over Sidbury and, generally keeping away from army installations or gunsites, as any unidentified low-flying planes usually got shot at, I would, ultimately, make my way back to my own 'private' airstrip, where I started to build my own plane. This flight would give me a bit of experience in flying before I finally took off again for my assault on the Third Reich! It seemed just as simple as that!

I was aware, only too well, that in the area were British and American fighter-planes, so, if things went wrong a hornet's nest would look tame compared with that lot buzzing around the place! What if I did manage to take off, and also land safely? I was bound to be found out some time, but the excitement of this whole adventure clouded my better judgment! Some people have to climb mountains, or sail the oceans, and so on, but my heart was in the heavens. (I did, in fact, nearly get there prematurely!)

It was almost eleven o'clock on the morning of the 13th December, 1942. This was to be the great day, and my brother John and I were getting very close to the airfield where I was to take-off and fulfil my wildest dream.

The prior arrangement between John and I was that, on selection of the plane we were to borrow, we would quickly take-off the tarpaulin covers and remove the tying-down ropes, manhandle the plane around and away, and to point it in the direction needed for a hasty take-off!

The field was not far away now and we had entered the wood which would be only a few yards from the planes. What if they had moved the planes away from the wood? The planes were quite a distance from the 'control tower' and from the light armoured tank where the sentry was usually stationed. There was always the possibility of German paratroopers, or spies and the like, attacking the field. This, dramatically, increased the danger of getting shot at by the trigger-happy guards!

We were both dressed in Home Guard Cadet uniforms, with army forage caps, unclipped and dropped down over our ears, and buttoned under the chin. Also, we were wearing khaki riding breeches, which the Aussie troops gave to us. In fact, although we did not know it, we looked, from a distance, very much like two Gerries, and that did not help matters a little later on that day!

The weather was very cold and the cloud ceiling, I think, was about four thousand feet, with light winds down the runway. We were crouched just inside the wood, with the planes now in view. It seemed that the sentries were well out of the way and we must soon make a move. It would be now or never! As I could not be sure that the planes would have fuel in, I had to go out first on my own to check which one had the most.

Suddenly, there were sounds approaching! We were about six feet inside the edge of the wood, hidden by the undergrowth, so we dropped onto our stomachs, afraid to breathe! I could hear my heart thumping in my ears! Was all the planning for nothing? We could just make out, through the trees, the figures of two American soldiers. They seemed to be deep in conversation and had now walked past where we crouched and were talking on towards the far end of the field. This was serious, as there was no way I was going to lock horns with sentries armed with Girand automatic rifles!

My mind began to whirl. It looked like the planning, the dreaming, was all for nothing. Already my mind, as I lay on the cold ground, was planning another form of 'attack' on another airfield, this one being the experimental air station at Boscombe Down, near Salisbury, eighteen miles from the spot where I lay. Now, I must admit, I had made a couple of 'recces' close up to Boscombe in the past but, as I had to do this after dark, and because of tight security, I did not fancy creeping around on an experimental station among different types of planes, possibly in questionable states of air-worthiness. I knew that this place was well defended, so only as a last resort would I try Boscombe Down. If I was going to steal a plane, as dangerous as that operation was, I also wanted to be sure that the plane I took would, as far as I could ascertain with my very limited knowledge of planes, be in good 'nick'.

John shook my arm, "Look!" he whispered. I glanced in the direction he was pointing. The two American sentries were at the far end of the airfield by now and, driving along the far perimeter, racing towards them, was a jeep. Had the sentries been suspicious after all and called up help? I was about to say to John "let's run and get the heck out of here . . ." but no, we waited. The jeep stopped on reaching the two Americans and the driver seemed to be talking to them. Suddenly, the sentries jumped on board and they all drove off. It now seemed that this was our chance, and I was going to do it my way after all!

As I lay on the cold ground that day, pondering as to when we would make a bolt to the airfield, my mind strayed back to my home village of Ludgershall, pronounced 'Luggershall', some said it had bugger-all, but to me it was our home, a place where most of my school pals, and myself, were born and, in a way, were proud of. It boasted an ancient monument – Ludgershall Castle. Oh, how many wonderful hours I had spent playing around its overgrown moats, climbing the ash and oak trees, shooting our home-made arrows at imaginary, mounted black knights, which I imagined still haunted the grounds and, sometimes, digging into the turf, hoping to find silver coins dropped in some bygone days. Yes, this place had a great history!

What a choice I had for adventure. A few miles west lay Stonehenge. I'm sure the reader is already well acquainted with its past. Then away to the east was Chute, with its Causeway and Hangman's Gallows (a place I could end up if I was caught!) and where, on a fine day, one could look down onto seven counties!

Much closer was Tidworth, just three miles away. It was there where all the 'big-time' was, for instance, a cinema – the Garrison Theatre – and a swimming pool up the road in among the army barracks. Only yards away was the site of the once world-famous Tidworth Tattoo, the Oval at the bottom of Station Road.

Then there was the River Bourne, a relatively minor river, where many times I had floated on oil-drum rafts from Collingbourne to Tidworth when the river was in flood, with John, and Clive and Eric Simpson.

Ludgershall was astride the main road which was, when I was a child, always busy with all kinds of traffic, mainly army transport. My father, in his earlier years, worked for the NAAFI. I remember the lovely, crispy bread he brought home sometimes from their bakery. Dad always owned a car or two, being a mechanic, one of which was constantly in bits (usually as a result of one of us pinching the parts!) and a great treat was the Sunday outing in the 'dicky-seat' of the French Le Rhone car, or whatever model was roadworthy at the time. Sometimes it was in my favourite car, the French Clement Talbot.

Tidworth Down Senior School was just outside the village, that is where I finished my school days. I loved that school because, mainly, it had a vast recreation and sports field and, of course, it had only recently been built with all the, then, latest classrooms and had wonderful views over the Downs.

My mother was always striving to keep us fed, clothed and in line. A tingle in the left ear was an ever-present reminder that she stood for no nonsense . . . John shook me back to reality!

"Come on, Jim, the coast is clear, let's go!"

The moment of truth had come! Now was the time when all the planning and bragging was to come to fruition, or to nothing! It seemed that my stomach was full of butterflies. Just fifty feet, maybe, separated me from the aeroplane. I still had time to back down, but I knew that once I was committed, there was no stopping. I am that kind of person, no way can I give up a challenge once I have committed myself.

We moved a few feet closer to the edge of the wood and now we could see in both directions. Not a soul in sight! Only the ten, or so, aircraft lined up in a neat row from left to right. It was now my job to go out to the planes and check each one for fuel, an easy task; because, in front, on the pilot's windscreen, on top of the engine cowling, was a steel spoke which had a float attached down below in the gas tank. This indicated the amount of fuel in the tank.

"Come on, Jim!" John was tapping my elbow, so off I crept, on all fours, from plane to plane until, at last, I found the aircraft which seemed almost full up with gas. On its nose, boldly stencilled was that name again, *Shirley Anne!* I had a good look around. The coast seemed clear and I gave John a quiet whistle. He emerged from the wood and joined me under the nose of the aeroplane.

Very quick action was now necessary. The plane was partly sheeted over and roped down to the turf. We both released the ropes, pulled off the covers, and proceeded to push the aircraft a few yards from the wood, always looking over our shoulders in case the sentries arrived back!

It was then, out of the corner of my eye, I spotted two girls at the end of the landing field. It looked like they were picking holly. I stared hard, trying to recognise them.

"That's all we need," I said to John, "look at those girls picking holly, they're bound to have seen us. Who are they? Can you make them out?" John stared hard.

"Yes, one of them is Jean Walsh. I can't quite see the other one. Yes, it's Zilda Long!"

Jean was about twelve years old and Zilda must have been about ten. They lived in Ludgershall and we knew them both. Zilda was my favourite, because of her lovely black hair, and her name had an electric sound to it. Jean had fair hair, and was the quieter of the two.

Zilda looked over the landing field to where she could see two young boys moving, furtively, about a U.S. Army plane.

"Look at those Stoodley boys, Jean, it looks like they are going to fly off!"

"No they won't, they can't fly a plane!" Jean replied, as she snapped off another stick of holly.

"I don't know about that!" said Zilda, "that Jim Stoodley was building his own plane and his Mum set it on fire. Look! They're turning it round, Jean. Let's hide down a bit and watch them! Look, he's trying to frighten us away! What's he shouting?"

"He's telling us to bugger-off," replied Jean, lowering herself down beside Zilda, shivering with cold.

Meanwhile, back on the airstrip the light tank sat, menacingly silent, at the far end of the field, it's short stubby-barrelled, 37mm Howitzer seemed to be watching our every move, pointing, seemingly, towards us as if daring us to steal one of its charges.

John climbed up into the observer's position, which was behind the pilot's seat, and I selected the magneto switch to the left magneto position, in order to prepare to start the engine. I checked, to be sure, that the ignition switch was in the 'off' position, and pumped the Ki-gas plunger three times to inject the fuel directly into the combustion chambers. I set the hand throttle, which was on the port side of the cabin, to one-quarter position.

"Strap yourself in, John, and hold the joystick back hard against your stomach". (This was very important to keep the tail on the ground.) "When the engine starts up I'll run round, clear of the propeller, and jump in the pilot's seat and take over the controls."

In our haste, however, I forgot to chock the wheels on the undercarriage! I moved around to the front of the plane, grasped the propeller, which I could barely reach on tiptoe, and realised that this was very dangerous! I had to remember to jump back, quickly, after each swing I made.

I had instructed John to switch on the ignition only when I shouted 'contact'. I looked around to see if anyone else was about. I could still see the two girls down the far end, watching us. I then reached up and, slowly, pulled down on the "prop" two or three times to suck in the fuel and rotated again on to the compression position. Then I shouted to John the magic word 'CONTACT'!

"Contact!" John shouted back, and switched on. Now, I had to pull down, hard, on the prop and, at the same time, back off, quickly, to avoid being struck by those deadly blades! I pulled down and stepped back. The engine misfired and kicked back, emitting lots of white smoke from the exhaust.

"Off ignition, John. Open the throttle one more inch. I've flooded the 'carb', I'll have to swing the prop a few more times and try to clear the excess fuel!" After a few turns I shouted again – "Contact, John!"

"Contact!" John replied, and I swung the prop and jumped clear. It was just as well I did, because the engine roared into life and the plane started to roll forward, slowly gaining speed! I grabbed the wing spar, ducked under and, like trying to jump aboard a moving bus, scrambled into the pilot's seat, reached over to the throttle and shut down the engine. During these few seconds, the plane was zig-zagging, madly, towards the centre of the airfield. We rolled to a halt, and the engine stopped!

"Why didn't you chock the wheels, you bloody fool?" shouted John.

"Come on, let's scarper!" I said, gasping for breath!

We both jumped out, leaving the ignition on, and ran like hell back to our hiding place just inside the end of the wood. All that engine revving and antics was enough to awaken the dead. We looked back to where *Shirley Anne* was left, sitting sedately, very alone, but in my eyes as much a challenge as ever!

We'll have to wait a bit, John," I said.

Minutes ticked by and still there was no sign of the sentries. Where the heck were they? Surely they must have heard us! But, after fifteen minutes or so, there was still silence and nothing on that airfield but the plane, and us!

"Look, John," I said, "are you still game?" "Yes, okay, but if we don't take-off this time I'm going back home, and that's final!" I felt as if he was losing the little bit of faith he had in me!

"All right, John, now look, the engine is a little warm, so, one final swing on quarter throttle should start her up, but let's walk slowly to the plane. You jump back into your seat, hold the joystick right back, the ignition is still on and I'll set the throttle on just less than a quarter, then I'll swing her up. If she starts up I'll jump in and we'll take off, and to hell with the expense!"

We started to walk, slowly, the three-hundred yards, or so, over to *Shirley Anne*. I had a nasty feeling that all hell would be let loose!

CHAPTER 11

The Flight

BEING a Sunday, and getting close to lunchtime, the thousands of American troops in Tidworth, and nearby Perham Down, were individually making their own plans. Some would be on duty, but most would go out on a pass. There was not a lot of entertainment for them. Andover was even miles south, a small, bustling town over the border in Hampshire. There were only the Odeon and Savoy picture houses, a couple of dance halls on a Saturday night, but plenty of pubs! The Americans liked beer, among other things, and they were a very friendly bunch of guys. It seemed that they were always trying to put on their best behaviour. Many local people did not realise that here were thousands of, mostly young, men thousands of miles from their own loved ones, only really wanting to help get the war over as quickly as possible, and get back to them. Many visited the pubs in Ludgershall. The Prince of Wales was one in particular. Some of the American troops from the Engineers were spending that particular Sunday working at the new vehicle park at the top of Station Road, Tidworth, and soon they would witness a sight they would not easily forget. Opposite was the edge of a large wood, mostly tall firs, densely packed together, stretching for several miles almost to Shipton Bellinger.

The soldiers were laying a tarmacadam surface over a large area. Soon it would be midday, time for chow! Nearly half-a-mile away, Mr Eddie Stoodley, Jim's dad, was going through a pile of paperwork in his office at the Depot. He had to work overtime today. He worked seven days a week. The hours had been a strain on his health, and so had Jim! "I wonder what the bugger's up to today," he thought, "God, that boy was a trial on his own. At least, when he was at work during the week, he could keep an eye on him, but Saturday and Sunday were danger days, that sod could be anywhere!" He remembered the day he caught him in the back of a Dodge command car interrupting a conversation between two tank convoy commanders on the short-wave transmitter, telling them to "get the hell off the air you goddam Yankee Doodles, I want to call my Ma!" For that he had kicked his arse all round the garage, but it made no difference, Jim was persistent, he just wanted to be living on the edge all the time, with no let up! Eddie Stoodley leaned back in his chair, looked at the clock on the office wall, almost 11.30 a.m. Yes, I suppose I've just got to keep my eye on him all the time, he thought. He reflected back to the time he sent him down to the tank repair shop for a course on the Wright Cyclone Radial engines on the Shermans and the V8 Cadillac engines on the light tanks, but he nearly electrocuted the chargehand and pulled the trigger on the foam fire extinguishers when the foreman fitter was laying in the engine compartment at the back of the tank, and on it went, so, he thought it best to keep him up at the motor pool with him!

John and I walked up to the plane. Here we were. Now we must make the final effort! John climbed up into the observer's seat. I set the throttle to one-quarter. I knew I'd left the ignition on, but I rechecked it. I also checked that the left magneto was on and walked around to the front of the plane. I had to start it up first go, I thought. I shouted to John "strap yourself in!" and reached up and grasped the propeller. Here goes, I thought, it's shit or bust! I pulled down with all my strength and stepped back. The engine sprang into life and just ran beautifully on a fast tick-over. I ran round clear of the propeller and jumped into the cockpit, sat in and looked all round the field. No-one in sight!

"Okay, John, here we go!"

I reached up and switched to both magnetos and the engine took on a more even note. I took over the dual control joystick from him, placed my feet on the rudder bars, got the feel of them pressing left and right, then centralised them, and prepared to take-off! The plane, at this moment was pointing towards the tank at the far end of the field, and I figured that I could take-off before I got that far!

I advanced the throttle to the three-quarter position and, with the stick pulled back, we began to roll forward! As the ground speed approached 30 knots, I eased the stick forward to the upright position and felt the tail lift up and held it steady whilst the speed increased to about 50 knots. I could now see through the front screen, and was terrified to see that we were getting very close to the light tank. I decided to shut the throttle to one-quarter, slowed down to about 30 knots, at the same time easing the joystick back as the tail lowered to the ground, and applied a bit of right rudder and the plane swung away to starboard, just missing the tank!

John shouted over my shoulder, "I thought you said you could bloody well fly it and look, you're taking off with the wind!" The wind-sock over the far side proved him right, so all I had to do was proceed back practically the way we had come. That would take us almost straight down the length of the field, so on we taxied, uneventfully.

"Third time lucky!" I shouted back to John, and with that, pushed the throttle wide open. I forgot to ease the stick back again and the tail quickly lifted and the propeller nearly hit the ground! I watched the artificial horizon and when the two lines levelled, I knew we were running level and I eased, slowly, back on the joystick. The airspeed was now about 50 knots and, slowly, we took off, just missing by inches the holly bushes at the end of the field!

I quickly glanced out of the side window, and saw two young girls looking up at us as we zoomed over their heads. Had they recognised us? I didn't think so, as our Home Guard Cadet forage caps were well pulled down over our faces!

I watched the ground fall away. I must keep straight and level, but let's get some safe altitude! So I let her climb, slowly, heading towards what I knew would be Andover, about seven miles away!

Zilda and Jean watch take-off.

55

CHAPTER 12

The Holly Pickers

WHEN John and I flew over the hedgerow at the end of the airfield, we were only a few feet off the ground and Jean and Zilda were astonished!

"I can't believe it!" gasped Jean, "they are in that plane and that Jim Stoodley's driving it!"

"Flying it, you mean!" answered Zilda "and the way he's just turned the corner in the sky, we aren't going to see them again!"

"Let's get our holly and go home, Zilda," said Jean, picking up her bunch.

They both hurried away, taking a last glance towards the plane, which was climbing and seemed to be heading towards Weyhill. It was very cold and by the time they arrived home it would be lunchtime.

"I'll see you later after lunch," said Zilda, leaving Jean near Mr Watson's farm. She only lived a few doors down from his place, and as she said goodbye to Jean, she saw Len Watton, who was one of Jim's schoolmates, at the end of the road. "Shall I tell him," she thought. "No, I'll tell my mum and no-one else." So, grasping her bunch of holly, she ran up the path to the bungalow and met her mum on the doorstep.

"Mum! Mum! you won't believe this! Do you know that Jim Stoodley?" she panted. "He's gone off in a Yankee plane, I've just seen him and John Stoodley. They were wobbling all over the sky. I called him back but he just waved and laughed and nearly crashed!" Mrs Long stood listening to her little daughter. "Don't be silly, Zilda, you know he can't fly! They're only boys. Now don't tell fibs, I've told you before about that!"

"I'm not fibbing, mum. We just ran from the polo field and the last we saw, he was going to Weyhill – sideways! You ask Jean Walsh, she was there. They shouted at us first, trying to scare us off, and that Jim told us to bugger-off!"

"You must not repeat those words!" admonished Zilda's mum. "Zilda, put the holly on the kitchen table." Zilda put the holly on the table, unhappy that her mum would not believe her story.

"Another thing, mum, if you don't believe me, he always pinches jeeps, and he has a tank hid somewhere over Tidworth, and he and his mates go in there and smoke cigarettes!"

Zilda in centre, age 9¹⁄₂ years, Jean on right, age about 11 years with GIs at gun emplacement on Perham Down, circa 1942. (Photo: Courtesy Zilda Harrop)

Mrs Long knew that Zilda had seen something. That lad did some really crazy things, but, fly a plane! But even she could not believe her story to be true. If it was, then she would soon hear more about it. Ludgershall was a small village and news travelled fast!

Zilda sat down and took off her shoes. They were muddy from her walk up to the polo field. That Jim Stoodley! she thought, he's spoilt my shoes making me run home. I'll tell his mum. Tears rolled down her cheeks. No-one ever believes me, she thought, but you wait and see! Jean was there, her mum will believe us!

The die was cast, here I was at last, airborne! I glanced at the altimeter, it told me I was flying at about 1,000 feet. In the back of my mind nagged a reminder to switch on the carburettor heater, because, if I went higher up, it would be colder and I did not want the carburettor icing up. That would mean big trouble and I had quite enough of that right now trying to keep the plane in the air, and on a reasonably level track!

Within a few minutes we were approaching Andover. I could see the large tower of McDougall's flour mills, fine on our port side and could easily see Andover railway station, which was alongside. I thought this was a good time to turn around and follow the railway-line back, which would lead me to Ludgershall, and where we lived. But, turning the aeroplane around was very different from flying in a straight line! Still, it had to be done, so I decided on a turn to port. Very gently, I applied left stick and left rudder and trying to move both in unison to avoid a side-slipping. I had made sure I kept my eye on the artificial horizon, so that I did not climb or fall on the turn. I managed this fairly successfully, at least I had no complaints from John, who was chatting away about the sights below, not in the least afraid! I was very nervous!

I shouted back to John, "We're heading back to Ludgershall along the railway lines, keep a sharp watch out for enemy fighters! I've got to watch where I'm flying" I had made a mental note before I took off to keep away from Southampton, as there was a balloon barrage there, and

The Polo Field, Perham Down, Wiltshire, 1994. Jim took off from this same landing strip on his epic flight, December 1942. (Photo: Courtesy Frank Gamble, 1994)

58

as I swung round on my new course, I caught a glimpse of them, briefly, on the far horizon. They were uncanny-looking objects and I did not relish getting my wings caught up in their wires!

As I left the Andover suburbs, I decided to lose height and hedge-hop, that would give me some hard experience, quickly, and also confidence, although John was not keen on flying low, his reason was that he could see a lot more scenery if we were higher! So I eased the stick forward, closed the throttle slightly, and down we went. The plane was skidding from side to side, so I applied a touch more throttle, steadied the rudder bars, as my legs were shaking a bit, and soon we were levelling out at roughly 200 feet.

I had to really watch ahead, constantly, for rises in the ground and electric pylon wires, etc. We passed over Weyhill and on we went towards Ludgershall. I increased the throttle slightly. Our airspeed was about 80 knots. John was talking over my shoulder. "Look, there's the water tower at Faberstown." We sped just over the top of it and lined the plane up on the railway-line and on towards Ludgershall railway station. Our house was about fifty yards from the railway-line and John shouted "Slow down, there's our house!" I banked to starboard, just in time to pass exactly over the house as my sister, Phyllis, was shaking a dust-mop from Mum's bedroom window, but she didn't see us! I noticed the air-raid shelter, which our family had dug, and thought that its camouflage was bad. If I could see it the Gerries could, so when, and if, I got down I'd really make it invisible from the air! (As if the Gerries were going to come especially looking for No.1 South View!)

We were past in a moment and up to the top of Central Street and could see Harvey Perry talking to Ray Collingson, and then we were over Crawlboys Farm. I banked hard to port, rather too sharply, and found myself very close to the plough-field below, so I lifted the nose slightly and just dead ahead I could see the local farmer walking ahead of me, guiding two horses, pulling a plough. Unfortunately, I frightened him, and his cart-horses, because they all scattered in different directions, and I was very sorry about that.

"For God's sake, go up higher!" yelled John.

I ignored him and picked up the railway-line again just outside Ludgershall, and headed towards Collingbourne Ducis. Looking ahead, I recognised so many landmarks, so I thought we would steer for Savernake, because I knew that in this area there was a railway tunnel, and it was when we reached the point where the rail disappeared into the tunnel, we about-turned and followed the railway back towards

Ludgershall. I felt a lot more confident by now and was travelling only a few feet above the rails and the telegraph poles, which were flashing by our wingtips! At every bridge we came to I had to lift the nose and we would just skim clear over the top and on to the next one! I suddenly remembered I had not turned the 'carb' heater off, so I did this immediately.

As I approached Collingbourne Bridge at Ludgershall, I could see, ahead of me, the special constable, who lived in Central Street. He was gazing straight at us from the bridge, leaning on the parapet. He was only about five foot four inches tall and he was known by all in Ludgershall as 'Six-foot'! Very nosy, he was, not an unusual habit for his occupation!

"Look, John, quick, down on the bridge – old Six-foot! Let's knock his hat off!"

"Yeah, go on, make him shit himself, Jim!"

I lowered the nose slightly, and just missed Six-foot by a few feet and, as we flew over him, John slid back the little window and shouted down at him "Get out of the way, you little short-arsed bugger," and as he slid closed the window, he knocked the throttle lever forward with his elbow, and the engine roared on full throttle! We burst out laughing and, as we glanced back Six-foot was picking himself off the road, minus his little peaked cap.

"That shook him!" chortled John, "it's about time he saw a bit of action, ain't it? Hee! Hee!"

By this time, I was approaching my old school, Tidworth Down Senior, very fast and low.

"Look!" I said to John, "there's the sports field and the bicycle sheds, and the air raid shelter . . ."

"Look out! Christ! Pull up quick!" John exclaimed. I instinctively eased back on the stick to gain more height.

"Bloody Hell! Just missed it!" John exclaimed and I realised we had missed the flag-pole on the school by a mere few inches and looked down, expecting to see the undercarriage rolling around the playground! I pushed the stick over to port, kicked the left rudder and executed a brand new type of bank, turn and side-slip, all in one! I knew now that I was pushing my luck past its limits and settled down to a climb, still on full throttle. I headed back out over Windmill Hill and over Tidworth Military Cemetery, and on up higher, climbing steadily all the time.

John seemed happy that, at last, we were gaining height and on we went, out over the firing ranges. Looking down below, everything seemed so small now! I checked the altimeter. Three thousand three hundred feet! Gosh! That's high! I thought, and began to make plans to return to Ludgershall and our field. I estimated we had been flying twenty-five minutes, maybe more, and it could be getting on for twelve o'clock, midday.

"How about dinner?" said John.

"All right," I agreed, impatiently, "we'll go back and land at Crawlboys on our own 'airfield'." (The place where I had been building my plane). I was preparing to turn round and make our way back, when . . .

V — R — O — O — M !!!

The whole plane shook violently, as a huge shape screamed past us from astern, diving over our flight-path!

"Christ! What the hell was that? Bloody Gerries?"

The whole aircraft shook violently, and I saw what appeared to be a Hurricane or Spitfire zoom right back up into the clouds, the shock of all this made me lose control of the aircraft for a few seconds, and I struggled to gain some sort of control again.

"Stupid sod," said John, "he nearly crashed into us, let's get the heck out of here, the Yanks may have seen us take-off and have raised the alarm."

Everything seemed to have happened so quick I did not see what kind of plane it was, I then decided it was time we started to make a turn and head back to the Long field, I made a slow turn back the way we had come, and then looked over my shoulder and could see Stonehenge behind so I thought we must be on the right course for Tidworth. Suddenly the engine started to misfire, and all sorts of spluttering sounds started to come from the exhaust, stone the crows, this is all we want I thought, and I could see the propeller slowing down through the windscreen and then the nose started to drop.

Immediately, I started to panic and pulled the stick back! The nose lifted, but I must have pressed the left rudder too, because the plane appeared to stop and slip sideways to port, straight down in a left-hand spin!

I instinctively realised that no plane will pull out of a spin unless you first gain enough speed to give enough lift, then gain enough air-speed to lift you out of the dive. So I immediately pushed the joystick forward, then over to starboard, at the same time centralising my rudder bars. However, as I pushed the stick a little too far over to starboard, she tried to start spinning in the opposite direction! I quickly centralised the stick, keeping it in the forward position, whilst all the time we were gathering speed! Slowly, the plane stopped spinning and we were diving near vertically!

I eased back the stick and the nose started to lift, and we levelled off. "I mustn't overdo this," I thought and, watching the artificial horizon, I tried to keep a very slight nose-up position. The propeller was just 'windmilling' and all kinds of spluttering and coughing was coming from the engine!

I knew we could not go far without full power and, looking below out of my starboard window, and just ahead, I could see Tidworth. Christ! What luck! Just by chance, we had headed back in the right direction! I looked at the altimeter, which read between 800 and 900 feet. I could see the Garrison Theatre picture-house, just distinguishable, near the crossroads. We were going to have a free balcony seat if we weren't careful – through the roof!

"Land on that new tarmac car park," shouted John. "Quick!"

I looked down and could see the tiny figures of soldiers, milling about, working on the park. We were still losing altitude, fairly fast, but we were well above the car park. The palm of my hands were soaking with sweat!

"No! We don't want to get caught, Dad's in the Depot down there!"

I had to make my mind up very quickly, while I was trying to keep the nose up slightly above the artificial horizon, and we were losing speed, very quickly!

Then I noticed, opposite the car park, was a large wood, several miles long. There were thousands of fir trees, tall, dark and menacing, but maybe our 'salvation', I thought. I reckoned I had enough speed and height just to bank carefully to starboard without stalling, to land on the treetops! From the air it appeared as one big carpet! This would be the one chance only, if any, and if I make a hash of it, that's our lot! and we'll get no dinner for a long time!

I gently eased her round and lined up with the trees, now only a few feet below us. As soon as we passed over the edge of the trees, I eased the stick forward, slightly, and suddenly remembered . . .

"Turn off the ignition switch!"

"Okay!" shouted John, "it's off!"

Just at that moment, the plane belly-flopped onto the trees, with a crash, and continued to skid along like a sledge, on the tops of the firs, branches flying in all direction, at the same time, tearing the floor away, so that, to my horror, I could see the ground whizzing past below me! Simultaneously, the port wing broke away with an ear-splitting crash!

The plane veered slightly to starboard and stopped, balancing precariously on the top of two or three trees, which had been decapitated!

The silence was deafening and we saw there, dazed and shocked, for a few seconds. Miraculously, the door was still intact, and I kicked it open, which was a foolish thing to do, because the plane rocked and slid slightly! I looked down at the ground, about fifty feet below, and thought "how the hell are we going to get out of this, because we're going to get nabbed if we don't do a bunk sharpish!"

Then it started! We could hear the wail of sirens!

"Come on, John!" I yelled, "we've got to get out of this, quick!" There was a warning smell of gasoline! The fear of fire was in my mind!

I climbed, gingerly, out of the cockpit, grabbed the nearest tree-trunk and, with great difficulty, climbed down as quickly as I could! I finally reached the ground, jumping the final six feet or so, walked back a few feet and looked up, instinctively, to see where John had got to. As I did so, I was covered with aviation octane fuel, which was dripping down the tree!

John was still sitting in the plane, leaning over the side, looking down at me, and shouting "Don't mind me, will you? I'm only here for the view! Do you want some toilet paper? You're a right sod leaving me up here!"

"Come on! Quick! The Yanks are coming!" I yelled, and as I did so, I glanced through the trees towards the edge of the wood, and could just make out scores of U.S. soldiers, swarming up in our direction, some with rifles, and there was an ambulance too! "They're quick off the mark," I thought.

I looked up again, to see John was climbing down and, when he was about ten feet from the ground, his clothing got hooked up on the short, stubby branches!

"Jump! For God's sake! They're here!"

He did just that! He jumped! He was lucky that the ground was soft and springy, as he hit it with a tremendous thud, rolled over, shook himself, and got to his feet. Then we bolted through the wood in the opposite direction to the approaching troops!

Now, there was one thing, in particular, I was good at and that was running. At school I was the one-hundred and two-hundred-and-twenty yards champion. I could also run five miles at a fairly good clip, so it was time to show John the quick way home, but by a roundabout route! John was hard on my heels as we left the scene of the crash!

After a couple of miles, I glanced around and, in the distant trees, I saw the remains of *Shirley Anne* up in the top, her tail-plane just visible. It was only then that I really felt the shock of the crash! How on earth did I put that plane up there, smash it up, and both of us get away without a scratch?

Eventually we reached home. By now, it was nearly two-fifteen, and Mum gave us a rocket for being late for dinner! Soon Dad would arrive home from work at the Depot. Did he know about the plane crash or not? We would not have long to wait to find out!

CHAPTER 13

The Consequences

SURE enough, Dad came home about three o'clock. John and I were sitting in the corner of the kitchen. "Hello, Phil," he said to Mum. "Had some excitement lunchtime!"

"Oh, what was that?" said Mum. Dad started to explain.

Well, we had a big plane crash up in the trees at the back of the Depot, and I sent two ambulances out, and a couple of wrecker trucks! The pilot must have bailed out, because they've searched all over for him, but can't find him! There's also a rumour that there may have been two of them in the plane and they could have been German agents! But we're not sure yet what the truth is!" I interrupted.

"What kind of plane was it, Dad?" knowing full well what type it was!

"I think it was a bomber," Dad replied, "an American fighter is supposed to have chased it over the firing ranges, but lost it! Where have you been today, Jim?"

"Oh, I've been out with John, cutting bows and arrows".

"Pity you didn't go out cutting firewood instead of buggering about like that. It's time you started to pull your socks up!" Dad continued to moan during his lunch, not knowing he was only six feet from the culprits!

"Yes, they'll get bloody shot if they get caught, if they are spies. Smashed it to smithereens they did! They must have bailed out, because no-one would have got out of that alive and, anyway, someone else is supposed to have seen two parachutes come down over Tidworth Oval!"

I was dying to tell Dad that it was not a bomber at all, and that there were no parachutists, but it was me and John who he was always telling to do something sensible, but I wasn't that stupid, so we decided to keep quiet!

I went back to work on Monday at the Depot, and everyone was talking about the 'Plane Crash', and I was, secretly, laughing at some of the fantastic stories that there were circulating, but after a few weeks, suspicion was beginning to be laid at my door!

For one thing, a lot of people knew that I had, for a long while, been building my own plane and, if, after a few weeks, no 'survivors' were found from the crash, then some people began to ask "where was Jim Stoodley on that particular day?"

One of those inquisitive types was a certain Detective Wyles. I had seen him a few times, watching us building our plane and, whilst he never really believed that it would fly, reminded me on a few occasions that I was not old enough to get a pilot's licence, and so on. It, naturally followed, therefore, that I would be prime candidate to lay the blame on, but he didn't have the proof and, anyway, no-one would ever believe a fourteen-year-old boy would steal a real aeroplane! Well, only, perhaps, Jim Stoodley might be crazy enough to do so!

It was towards the middle of January, 1943, that Mr Eddie Stoodley was in his office at the motor pool. It was almost lunchtime and in walked two Special Enquiry Agents attached to the U.S. Army, who are investigating the theft of the plane, and would Mr Eddie Stoodley go and ask Jim if he took the plane or not?

I was in the Colonel's car in the garage opposite his office when Dad came in.

"I want a serious talk with you, Jim!" he said, ominously. "Now I want you to answer me truthfully, yes or no to my question. Did you and John steal that plane?"

"Yes, Dad," was the automatic answer.

Now, my Dad was the finest man I knew and, whilst he was very strict, I found him fair to a fault, and he knew that, at the end of the day, he could rely on me to ultimately tell the truth. I knew he was proud of me, but he had to put a front on.

"Do you know who is in my office?"

"No, Dad."

"Well, I'll tell you. The bloody FBI, that's who! They've finally caught up with you and I'll tell you this much, you'll be shot at dawn, like a spy! Don't you think I have enough problems, without you adding to them?"

"I'm sorry Dad, I only took it to make you proud of me."

"Proud of you! I'll bloody disown you! Who are we supposed to be fighting, the Germans or the Yanks! They're on our blasted side aren't they, you stupid sod?"

But Dad knew that I was far from being a stupid sod and, secretly, he was proud of me and would stand by me, come what may, just as he would any of his other thirteen children.

"You'll have to go to court, you know," Dad said, "and just think of all the disgrace you will bring on the family." I felt pretty ashamed of myself.

I went to court on the 6th February, 1943, at Ludgershall Juvenile Court. The small village courthouse was packed with many reporters and spectators, who overflowed out into the yard. There were U.S. Army personnel present and most of them came up to me and shook my hand. Zilda and Jean were there too, and I gave them a sly wink!

The summonses against me were as follows:
Flying an aircraft in time of war without:
a certificate of airworthiness;
a certificate of insurance;
a pilot's licence;
a certificate of competency to fly;
flying an aircraft in time of war without permission of the Secretary of State for Air, etc.

The court took a lenient view and bound me over for twelve months. An American colonel paid substantial costs for the damage on my behalf.

As the Spring of 1943 progressed into Summer, I began to get restless again for adventure! The summers on the Plain seemed to be better than anywhere else. Gosh! How I wished I was older so that I could go and fight!

More Americans were pouring into Salisbury Plain and, with many armoured divisions, there were plenty of tanks of all types! I carried on working at the Depot, still getting into minor scrapes. Colonel Richland used to have a chat with me when I called at his office with messages, so things couldn't be so bad.

On my spare evenings, when possible. I used to go up to the U.S. Army barracks at Perham Down and also Tidworth. I was fascinated by their crap-games and baseball. I used to borrow a rifle from them and show them how we presented and sloped arms. They, in turn, gave me instruction on their methods.

They used to gather round in the billet whilst I told 'true' ghost stories! The Americans seemed awestruck by them, and they split their sides with laughter when I said I thought the Mason-Dixon Line was a railroad company, when in reality it was the imaginary dividing line between the North and South at the time of the Civil War!

I used to look forward to chow-time, as they would supply me with a mess kit and I would queue up with them in the mess hall. Boy! What a line-up of food there was! I could not get used to their habit of splashing a dollop of jam on their potatoes, but I made up by getting ice-cream. I knew that this time of my life, which I was experiencing, would not last forever and, always aware of this, I tried to live out every minute of it, being war-time, anyway, there seemed to be no tomorrow!

CHAPTER 14

Not A Bad Bunch Of Guys

U P to now, I had met thousands of GIs of all types. Some were from the 1st, 2nd, 3rd and 10th Armoured Divisions, also many from the 29th Infantry and 82nd Airborne, mostly on a casual basis. There were, also, many other divisions I no longer remember.

I used to sit for hours in different barracks at Tidworth and Perham Down and listen to their stories of 'back home'. A lot of people thought the Yanks were a lot of boasters, but, after seeing the quality of their military equipment, even the most biased would agree they had a lot to boast about ! That the Americans were 'oversexed and over here' was a regular remark heard in England during the war, but my own opinion was that our lads, when they were serving abroad, certainly didn't all sit in the barracks every night, and I am sure that if it came to question-time they would be the first to admit that they were not the slightest bit different!

I, personally, liked and got on well with the GIs because they were on our side, they were friendly and were doing their best to help us, and themselves, to beat the Germans. The fact they were better paid than our troops was a cause of jealousy, but the residing British Government could have been blamed for the low pay which our forces had to suffer, so miserably, at that time.

Sure, some GIs drank a lot, so did our boys, but the pressures and anxieties, brought about by total war, do strange things to all men and women and, invariably, the fact that men, mostly young, are away from their loved ones and their own country tends to bring about over-indulgence in different degrees.

Many confided to me about their personal domestic problems. Many worried about their wives and girlfriends too, back home on their own without their menfolk. I have seen many a good soldier cry! That is a pitiful sight, particularly for a fourteen-year-old boy. I must admit I have been bewildered, and upset, by all this. I used to do my best, in my humble way, to talk to them about the thousands of others in similar circumstances and that, one day, they would return to a world of peace. What a lovely word that was! So much seemed to be taken for granted in peacetime but, in future, we all prayed that a war like this, or any war, would not be allowed to happen again.

The American soldiers always liked to dress up smartly and go out on the town. He would sit in the barrack room and press his best uniform till you could cut yourself on the creases! His brown leather shoes used to glow over his silk socks! He would look in the mirror, tilt his forage cap to the correct angle and fill his pockets with 'ammunition' for the night out, that usually being a couple of packs of Lucky Strike, Camel or Chesterfields, a couple of sticks of candy, a couple of french-letters and enough green-backs to tempt the evils of the night!

He usually had a favourite pub to go to, as he liked the good English beer, and could drink a lot of it! Sometimes he would drink too much and end up drunk as a newt, or he would meet one of the local girls and, perhaps, it would be a drink, or a movie, and a one-night-stand, it all depended on the girl, the guy, or opportunity!

Why did the Americans always make a beeline for all the ancient monuments? Simply because they had no real old ones back home. I remember going up to Stonehenge with several GIs in a truck. They walked round and round the place, speechless at this giant man-made wonder! Each one had his own version of how the stones had arrived there. One wise-guy from the Bronx said they had been shipped over from the States, another put forward his theory that they had always been there, which had a ring of possibility, and another said simply "It sure beats the balls off of me!" which, probably, accounted for the painful expression on his face!

The S.O.S. (Service of Supply) company had many negro drivers and a few used to tell me the way they were treated back home. I could not believe some of the stories I heard about the miserable life they were living but, to many, the war brought relief, in-as-much as they came to a much more relaxed country that, at the time, had no positive racial problems like America. They could walk out with white girls, which infuriated the other GIs very much! They could ride on mixed buses and go to mixed cinemas, etc.

The GIs would, on a fine evening, sit around the Triangle in the centre of Ludgershall. Nearby was the Crown Hotel, a nice homely place, next to the Fire Station. Above the Fire Station, on the hose-drying tower, was that dreaded air-raid siren, and across the road, the barbers, then our favourite sweet-shop and, taking up the next block, E. E. Roys Furniture Shop, which was always a mysterious kind of place, with a lot of glass along the front of the showrooms. The strange thing was, there never seemed to be a salesman in sight but, as soon as you entered the shop, they seemed to drop down on you from the rafters, like vampires! If I ever went in there, it was always the usual "sod off Jimmy!" I used to think I'd come back one day and buy the shop.

Along the way, and opposite, was the Post Office and Bakery of Frank Rawcliffe. We would help him pull his bread hand-cart up Central Street sometimes, until he realised the cart was always lighter at the top than when it started at the bottom, and he'd clip our ears many a time!

Still, Ludgershall was really a great place to live in. The people were all 'stick by you' types. If anyone had problems they would help each other out, except me, as everyone knew mine were unsolvable!

We had a nice sports field up at Astor Estate, and a very large recreation ground up Deweys Lane. The local council really looked after us youngsters and old ones alike.

The surrounding countryside was immaculate, that was the only way one could describe it. The fresh air, the colour and the environment was so relaxing, and I am sure that many a GI who had the good fortune to call on Ludgershall would have been captivated by its beauty.

Yes, we were proud of our village and surrounding Wiltshire. I would have willingly given my life defending it against the enemy, that's why I was always armed to the teeth out on Windmill Hill. The Gerries would pay dearly if they ever wanted my 'back yard'!

The Prince of Wales was another favourite with the GIs, near the GWR Station, a station which saw the comings and goings of thousands of troops of many nations, through two world wars!

Ludgershall lost many of its dearest sons in those terrible wars and is much poorer from that great loss. On the memorial at the Triangle are their names. I shall never forget their great sacrifices. Ludgershall is a very lucky place to live in.

Of course, the presence of first the French from Dunkirk at Ludgershall Station, then the Aussies, then the GIs, upset the steady heartbeat of the village, but we all knew that they had come to help us do a job and, apart from just a few dissenting voices, broadly speaking, we all tried to get on as well as we could. A few local girls married GIs and, after the war, we would soon try to return to normal but, alas, that could never be, because war leaves many scars, broken homes and hearts, new faces arrive, new housing goes up, and the village loses its old charm. Not that Ludgershall is poorer for that.

The Railway Station was, in time of war, a very important junction. Men and war supplies were steamed in from Andover, off-loaded for the immediate area and some shunted up to Tidworth to the large Ordnance Depot, and numerous camps in the area of Salisbury Plain.

A few months after the arrival of the U.S. Army *en-force* and, thereafter, the tremendous back-up of war material, it took less than an expert to see who would eventually win this war, but it was to be a long, hard slog. Many a GI who passed through the village never returned to his homeland.

A lot of GIs didn't know what a village was until they came to England. Very few of them, who I personally met, had a chip on their shoulder. After Pearl Harbor, most of the Americans felt that the war in Europe was as important as the one in the Pacific.

The guys I worked with never once shirked or dodged the column. Many worked double duties to load and unload supplies. Technicians prepared vehicles and various equipment endlessly, in shifts, day and all night. Hitler had started something he couldn't finish! The Yanks were coming, Bosch Boys, look out! As Admiral Yamamoto said after Pearl Harbor "I fear we have stirred a sleeping Tiger!" That was the understatement of the century.

For all the horror of war, which millions suffered, I felt honoured to have had the pleasure of meeting, and working with, so many American servicemen. To me it was a Walt Disney wonderland of every possible dream crammed into a few short years. That I came through all my escapades and scrapes unscathed was a miracle in itself!

I believe that when you are born a star is created in the heavens and, as that star travels through the galaxy, so we travel through our lifetime. When that star falls, so do we. So lies our fate!

CHAPTER 15

Miss Bobby From Biddesden House

I HAD tried lots of things as a young boy, but I had not had much experience riding horses, and I had this sudden urge, brought on by a few GIs telling me about their ranches back home in the States, so, not to be outdone, I decided to borrow a horse and go up to the barracks at Tidworth and show off a bit and try to impress the Yanks I knew there.

There were plenty of horses around Ludgershall, but getting someone to lend me one for the day was easier said than done, as most would not trust me to return it in one piece! But I could see a chink of light! I suddenly remembered a friend of mine, Desmond Guinness from Biddesden House, a lad about by age who was the son of Bryan Walter Guinness who, in 1944 became Lord Moyne.

I knew Desmond fairly well, but only saw him on rare occasions when he was on vacation from his studies. His stepmother, Elisabeth Guinness, later Lady Moyne, was a very beautiful lady, with long dark hair and refined classical features. Their grand house, which they bought in 1931, was set in lovely surroundings. Desmond was very handsome, had impeccable manners and a great personality. I always enjoyed his company and, on one or two occasions, he used to show me around the house, which had secret panels and passages, making it always very interesting!

The main hall, which was very imposing, had a large painting on the wall of the man who built the house, General John Richmond Webb. It is said that he was rather upset because someone else got the credit, at first, for winning the battle of Wynendael, one of the Marlborough battles and came, sulking, to Biddesdden where he built this very imposing house. The painting depicts General Webb sitting astride his horse in that battle. Years later, when the house was sold, the painting was removed from the house and, until it was brought back, it is said that the inhabitants were kept awake by the sound of hooves clattering up and down the large wooden staircase. When the painting was returned to its place in the hall the 'haunting' stopped, so that General Webb still looks down, seeming content and, nowadays, all is quiet!

To return to the horse I needed. Lady Moyne owned some pure-bred

Arabians but, generous as she was, I could not see her allowing me to loan one of them but, at worst, I might have the loan of a cart-horse! Anyway, I decided to go and see if Desmond could make any helpful suggestions.

It was difficult to catch him at home and, to be honest, I was a little afraid of seeing Lady Moyne because I had asked one of her nursemaids for a date on several occasions, without success, and the last time I asked her she threatened to tell Lady Moyne, so I thought it prudent not to ask her any favours, except as a last resort!

One night in the week I went down to see Desmond and, luckily, I found him at home. I walked up the long drive leading to the house, the gravel crunching under my step, glancing, nervously, up at the windows, then walked on around to the side of the house to the servants' entrance and rang the bell. I could hear footsteps and soon the door opened. A maid looked, inquiringly, down at me.

"Who is it you want?" she asked. I tried to look important.

"I'm Jim Stoodley. I have come to see Desmond. Is he in please?"

"Just one moment," she replied, "I'll go and see!" Off she went, and very soon Desmond appeared at the door.

"Oh, hello, Jim. What can I do for you?"

"Sorry to trouble you, but I am a bit desperate for the loan of a horse next Sunday, Desmond. I want to go up to visit some Yankee friends of mine at Tidworth, and they are all bragging about the horses they have back home, so I wanted to show the flag, if you get my drift!" Desmond rubbed his chin and began to walk with me down towards the stables.

"Well, Jim, I think the only way I can help is to loan you Miss Bobby. She's a chestnut mare, getting on a bit, but if you take her carefully, you are welcome to her. What do you think, Jim?"

"Oh, she'll do fine, Desmond," I replied delightedly, "would it be okay if I come up on Sunday in the morning, about nine-thirty?"

"That will be all right, Jim," he replied, "I'll see you at the stables then, and I'll fix up the riding tackle for you, then you will be all set for the day out!" With that, I bade him goodbye and made my way back to Ludgershall, feeling very happy.

When the appointed day arrived, the early morning sun was warm on my cheeks. I went down to Biddesden House, which was a two-mile walk. As I left the outskirts of the village, I passed Len Watton, who used to go to school with me at the Tidworth Senior School.

"Hello, Jim. What's on this morning then?" he asked, wondering what I was doing out so early, and at that end of the village!

"All right, Len. Oh, I'm going out for a ride up to the camp, on a horse!"

"Where are you getting the gee-gee from then, Jim?"

"You know Desmond Guinness? He's lending me one of the best horses in the stables! His Mum said it's okay, and I'm going to give the Yanks a demo on good riding!" Len looked a bit disbelievingly at me.

"I think you're pulling my leg, Jim. They wouldn't lend you a horse; you can't ride one."

"Well, Len, you just watch me coming galloping up this hill in half-an-hour and, if you're still here, I'll give you a go!"

"Yeah! I'll believe that when I see it, Jim! But I will have a go if you do show up!"

"Okay, Len! See you later. Cheerio!" and off I went, whistling, on to Biddesden.

I arrived on time at the stables and, true to his promise, Desmond was there already, with Miss Bobby.

"Good morning, Jim," said Desmond, as he turned around and saw me walking towards him. "Here, Jim, I'll introduce you to her."

We walked around to the front of the horse and Miss Bobby seemed very placid indeed.

"Now, Jim," Desmond went on, "she is good in traffic and I have fed her this morning, so just be sure you give her a drink or two during the day and I will see you later on. All right, Jim?"

"Yes, that's fine, Desmond. I'll be back at teatime," then with a little bunk-up from Desmond, I was up in the saddle.

"There you go, Jim. Have a nice day out."

"Thanks, again," I replied and, at a steady pace, I made my way out of the yard, onto the lane, back to Ludgershall.

It was not too long a ride and I soon arrived at the outskirts of the village. I had not seen Len. Perhaps he had got tired of waiting, or he, probably, did not believe me, anyway! I rode into our garden and all the family came out of the house to make a fuss of the horse. My brother, Bob, was on leave from the Black Watch Regiment and he climbed up on the back of Miss Bobby. As he climbed up, his Scottish kilt blew over his head, and all the girls who were watching received an eyeful! At last, everyone knew that he didn't wear anything underneath, and they all gasped! Bob went as red as a beetroot and started to ride around the garden. When he was fed up I took over and made my way into Tidworth, and soon arrived at Brimstone Bottom, where Frank Gamble, another schoolmate, was digging his front garden. He looked up as he heard the sound of the horse and was quite amazed to see me up in the saddle.

"Well, Jim," he exclaimed, "I've seen everything now! Is that your horse?"

"No, Frank, I've just borrowed her for the day from Desmond Guinness."

"Oh, yes," he replied, "that's good of him, isn't it? You do have some posh friends, don't you, Jim?"

"Well, you know how it is, Frank! I do like to think that, and you sure can rely on them to help you out when you want a favour, can't you?"

"Yes, I suppose that's true, Jim," he agreed. "Anyway, Jim, have a nice ride out to Tidworth, and mind you don't fall off!"

"See you, Frank!" I shouted as I rode on to the barracks.

I was feeling pretty cocky by now and I started to sing a song:

> *Roll along covered wagon, roll along,*
> *By the turn of your wheels I sing a song,*
> *City ladies may be fine*
> *But get that girl of mine,*
> *Roll . . .*

Ouch! Miss Bobby turned her head and bit my foot, as though to protest at the row! It was a good job I had strong boots on, but it still hurt a bit. I had better shut up, I thought, even the bloody horse doesn't appreciate my singing. Sure enough, as long as I didn't sing, Miss Bobby plodded on as normal!

The sun was quite hot now and I could see the U.S. Army camp just ahead. I rode up to the billets, where my friends were and a few spotted me was I approached.

"Hiya! Jimmy!" one shouted. "Where did you get that old mare" Another shouted, "Here's Tom Mix" and "Jimmy, you're facing the wrong way, aren't you?" Out of the corner of my eye I could see a GI sergeant known as 'Father Kelly', ambling up with his usual bottles under his arm!

"Hi, Jim. You look a right dude sitting up there." I wasn't sure what that meant, so I ignored the remark!

"Hello, Kel." I replied, "How you doing?"

"Not too bad. Where did ya get the mare?"

"It belongs to a wealthy friend of mine, Kel. The man from the big brewery in Ireland."

Kelly made out that he was inspecting Miss Bobby and, as he walked around the front of her, she lifted her head up with a jerk, as if to avoid his breath!

75

He continued to go on and on: "Yes, I knew a gal back home. Her Pa had a whole string of horses. I used to go out on the range many a time with her. She sure was a beauty! The gal I mean, Jim! Yeah, but her old man didn't care much for me, in fact, he tried to run me off one day and I had to move, because he had a goddam Winchester rifle! Told me not to set foot on his land again. Yeah! He was one mean son-of-a-bitch."

"I didn't wonder why he ran off, Kel," I replied, "if you used to drink like you do now, and you've had a few today by the looks of things!"

"Aw, shit! Jimmy, I only had a few beers after Mass. Just to wash the Holy bread down!" and with that remark, he sauntered off to the barracks!

I secured the horse to the nearest hedge and went into the billets. Most of the GIs were sitting down on their beds, reading or writing letters home to their loved ones. I walked down the rows of beds, chatting to a few I knew, who I worked with in the Depot. I could hear Kelly singing hymns down the far end. As usual, everyone felt it best to leave him alone when he had consumed a few beers!

Near the end of the hut there was a young soldier who was crying. I asked S/Sgt Single what was the matter with him.

"Oh, Jimmy, that's a regular thing every Sunday. He just gets homesick, I guess. Thinking of his Ma and family back home. We just don't take any notice of him and, by chow-time he's okay again!"

"Oh!" I replied, and I went over to the bed where he sat sobbing.

"Hi, Shultz!" I said, "like a Lucky Strike?" Shultz looked up, surprised that someone should talk to him, wiped his eyes, sat up and straightened his collar.

"No, I don't smoke, thanks," he said and looked embarrassed.

"Do you ever ride a horse back home?" I asked.

"Sure do!" he replied, "really miss my horse over here!"

"Well, would you know much about horses?" I asked.

"Yeah!" Shultz replied, "Spent my life with them. Know them from head to tail. We must have fifty or more back in Oregon!" Shultz seemed to be feeling better now, and much recovered.

"Would you like to see my horse and give me your opinion of her, as you seem to be such an expert on them?" Shultz looked at me, surprised, his eyes lighting up a bit.

"You got a horse?"

"Well – er – yes, outside the door."

"Outside the door? Gee! Mind if I take a look?"

"No. Come right on out and tell me what you think, Shultz."

He got up and out we went to where Miss Bobby was tethered. Shultz's eyes lit up.

"Shit, man, that's a lovely horse, something like the one my Grandpa owned years ago when I was just a kid!" He walked up and started talking and patting Miss Bobby.

"Here, jump up, Shultz, and have a ride. I'll walk up front and we'll go out for a couple of miles." I was hoping this would get him out of his fit of homesickness a bit. So we set off up towards the ruins of Tidworth Castle.

It was a lovely afternoon. The birds were singing and the war seemed a million miles away. Shultz was chatting on about his folks back home, worrying whether he would ever see them again. About his sister, who was crippled and whom he missed taking riding so much.

"Yeah, I guess you Limeys have had a hard time in this war," he went on.

"Well, it's not that bad," I replied, "when you know you are going to win in the end, it doesn't matter if things get difficult."

"I wish I was as sure as you we're going to win," Shultz replied, "them Germans are going to take some beating, ain't they, Jim?"

"Well, what with you GIs and all your resources and brains, and us English with all our guts, we'll win that is definite!"

"Guess you're right, Jim. Yeah, guess you're right," mused Shultz, still sitting up on Miss Bobby like a professional, reins lightly held in his fingers. "Sure is a nice mare, Jim. Great of you to give me a break like this."

"I know it is!" I replied, "think nothing of it! When I meet you maybe, back in the States, after all this is over, you can take me out on the Prairies and we can hunt Buffalo, eh Shultz?" He laughed out loud.

"Yeah, maybe so, maybe so."

We looped around the old castle ruins and head back to the barracks. I must soon head back to Biddesden House and get Miss Bobby fed and bedded down. We arrived back at the barracks and it was soon apparent that Shultz was feeling his usual self.

"Gee, thanks, Jim, for a real nice break."

"You're welcome, Shultz. I'll have to get back now. I'll see you at work in the Depot tomorrow. Okay?"

He waved goodbye and off I went back through Perham Down and on to Biddesden House. I met Desmond near the main entrance.

"Have a nice ride, Jim?" he asked, as he walked up with me to the stables.

"Yes, thanks, Desmond. A grand day. Went to Tidworth, but a funny thing happened when I was singing, she turned her head and tried to bite my toe!"

"That's strange!" he replied, puzzled, "never know her to do that before!"

"Well, when I stopped singing she seemed okay!"

"Oh, that must have been why she tried to bite you, Jim, she couldn't stand the pain!" he laughed.

"Yes, I suppose so, Desmond," I replied ruefully, "I'll see you again sometime," I called, as I made my way off home.

"Okay, Jim, anytime. You're welcome. Goodbye!"

I started walking to Ludgershall and felt fairly stiff after sitting in the saddle nearly all day. Not a bad experience, although I think I'd rather drive!

CHAPTER 16

Death In The Tank Shop

FOR us young apprentice fitters working in the vast tank shop, there was always plenty of excitement and, also, lots of hidden dangers. With all the very heavy Sherman tanks, and various armoured vehicles, one had to be constantly on the alert for vehicles reversing, or overhead cranes trundling their swinging heavy loads over one's head, by operators who always seemed to be in a hurry to deliver their loads to different locations in this workshop.

I suppose there would be about a hundred Shermans and other vehicles at one given time, undergoing some sort of repair or modification, and this presented a continuous hive of activity twenty-four hours a day, even though we young lads only worked days from 8 am. until 5 p.m. But work we did, as a team, to help get these war machines out to the various units awaiting their delivery.

Some days, I would team up with U.S. technicians, removing tank turrets. That was a risky job, because when the turret was being replaced I had to stand inside the tank underneath the turret while it was levered onto the large steel ring which, in turn, had to have many bolts and nuts pushed through and tightened up with a large heavy wrench. Then, perhaps, at other times, we would remove an engine, and so it would go on, week after week.

The tanks were all parked side by side in long lines, with only two feet between the sides and it was on the occasion when I had to help fit and weld extra armoured plates on the sides of the Sherman that I witnessed a terrible accident!

These armoured plates were about four feet long, two feet wide and one inch thick. The main reason they were being fitted was because it was found that in the Western desert, many of these tanks were blowing up after direct hits on the high sides, near the ammunition locker for the 76mm gun, and this was causing not a little worry to the crews! Quite frankly, an extra inch did not make one iota of difference when a shell from the German 88mm high velocity gun struck home, but it made the crews feel that much safer, those who had not had the unpleasant experience of getting shot at by these deadly and very accurate guns!

The German 88mm gun was first designed as a high altitude anti-aircraft gun and the Germans soon realised that it was easily adaptable as an anti-tank weapon and, later in the war, was fitted to the large Panzers and outclassed all Allied armour, until the Sherman was fitted with a seventeen-pounder, long-barrelled gun which, in turn, gave the Gerries the shits whenever it appeared on the battlefield. In fact, the British army (who made the conversion and renamed it the Firefly) would always have at least one or two Fireflies with a squadron of Shermans, to scout ahead and take on the heavy German armour; but let's go back to the job in hand in the tank shop.

I was assisting a local English welder, on this particular day, to secure these large pieces of additional armour to two tanks. We waited while the overhead crane started to bring its load over the top of everything, and everyone working below. What would happen was this; when the armour plate was directly over where we stood the operator would be signalled to lower the plate slowly down, and manoeuvre it alongside, and level to the chalk-marks on the side of the Sherman. He would, then, be signalled to stop when this was attained, and the plate quickly held by a telescopic jack resting against the tank alongside, two feet away. We would then weld-tack the four corners of the armour, securely enough, then the holding chains would be released and swung clear. A welder would then come behind us and completely weld it in place, while we moved on to another tank and repeated the process all day, maybe for several days.

This day proved to be fatal for my co-welder, who did not stand back far enough as I did, and as the plate was hovering ten feet above, he would not heed my advice to walk back a few steps.

Without warning, the chain snapped! The plate fell and hit him, edge on, like the blade of a guillotine, the sheer weight crushed him to the concrete floor and cut him almost in two above his waist. Only his heavy one-piece overalls hid the terrible injuries!

For a moment, I stood, as if glued to the spot, not able to utter a word or move a step. Then, suddenly, I was able to release a shout for assistance. I rushed forward to help, trying to lift this awesome thing that had pinned him down. I could do nothing but step back and watch the men who had raced from all directions and started to lift aside the armour plate.

Bill lay there, unmoving. On his face was a look of horror which I shall never forget. A doctor soon arrived and pronounced Bill dead and they carried him away on a crude stretcher. I stood there, watching, thinking I could have been dead too!

I went home that evening a very shaken young man. It showed that danger, and even death, lurked around every corner!

CHAPTER 17

Colonel Richland, C.O. Tidworth Depot

T HE Colonel had spent a hectic morning. He had just left a meeting with his various officers in command from different departments in the depot.

Major Hunnicut of the Artillery 'shop' was pressing him for more men to unpack, clean and assemble the new artillery pieces that had arrived from the States. Captain Barrett from the Tank 'shop' had also been badgering him for more spare parts for the scores of Sherman tanks and White halftracks that were his job to prepare for waiting units at various training centres.

He sat down at his large desk and called his secretary: "Eileen! Is there any coffee?" Eileen was a small, but pretty, English girl, employed, like dozens of other English personnel, at this very large complex.

"Yes Sir, I will get you a cup right away."

The Colonel glanced at his desk. His eyes wandered around and out through the window. He could see the hills surrounding Tidworth. So much green, he thought, not like the part of Texas which was his home back in the States. He was six-foot four-inches tall, a bronzed, well-built man, very young-looking, although he was, in fact, in his early fifties. A fair and patient man to all he had under his command. Eileen came in with his coffee.

"Here you are, Sir." The Colonel leaned back and yawned.

"Gee, thanks, Eileen. You sure do make a good cup of coffee . . ." Eileen interrupted:

"Excuse me, Sir. I have a report here from the Inspector of the English Depot Police. You know the young lad who stole the plane? They are complaining in strong terms about his behaviour again!"

Colonel Richland choked on his mouthful of coffee and spluttered it all over his desk!

"Hell! Not him again! Why I tolerate that guy for so long, God knows!"

He was thinking, that Jim Boy had caused more uproar in this Depot, and out of it, than the Germans had! He had already appeared on his behalf in the court, and paid his costs, when he smashed up a U.S. plane. Why did he stick up for this guy?

"Bring me another coffee, Eileen. Here, give me the report." He opened it and read it slowly:

Dear Sir,

May I respectively bring your attention to the following. My Sergeant and Constables on duty at various points around the Depot have reported to me that Jim Stoodley has been seen driving a Sherman tank up the north end of the Depot, and nearly ran over a constable who signalled him to stop.

He was also stopped on two other occasions driving a halftrack personnel carrier and deliberately splashed the constable with muddy water . . .

The Colonel laughed, silently, to himself and thought life would be kind of dull without him around. The report went on:

Would you please confirm if Jim Stoodley has your authority to drive in this Depot. This lad is, as you may already be aware, only fourteen years. When questioned he said you were a 'mate' of his and he had your permission to drive anything in the confines of the Depot complex.

The Colonel smiled to himself and thought, "that little guy has got a nerve."

"Eileen, get on to Mr Robert Stoodley in the Motor Pool. Tell him to send his son down to report to me at 3.30 p.m. this afternoon – on his own! I'll have to have a good talk with this Jim Boy and straighten him out, otherwise I'll end up getting fired myself!"

It so happened that when my Dad received this message, I was polishing the Colonel's personal staff car and had found cigars and cigarette tobacco and papers inside.

"Jim! Jim! Come here!" Dad shouted, as he walked over towards me. "What the hell have you been up to again?" I looked at my Dad with that usual well-trained expression! "Well, Colonel Richland wants to see you in his office at 3.30 p.m. Sharp!"

"Okay, Dad, I'll be there."

This will give me the chance to return his cigars and fags, I thought, I want to keep on the right side of him, after all, he's the big wheel around here, so I'll do plenty of hand-shaking and show him how honest I am. Poor Dad, I didn't realise it at the time, but he had plenty of worrying to put up with, without me piling it on!

I knocked at the Colonel's office and his secretary admitted me. I was one minute early by my Bulova watch. The Colonel liked punctuality, cleanliness and respect, and I made sure I showed him these qualities!

"He will see you now," his secretary said, opening the door, and there he was, large as life, the God of Tidworth Depot!

I walked up, smartly, the few feet in front of his desk, stood to attention, chin up, chest out, and said, "Jim Stoodley reporting, Colonel, Sir!"

Colonel Richland sat there, hands clasped and elbows resting on his desk, his blue eyes gazing straight at me.

"Now Jim, sit down," he said.

"Excuse me, Colonel Sir," I said, hurriedly forestalling him, "I have cigars and tobacco you left in your Chrysler."

"Put them on the desk." He indicated a point near a piece of paper, where, even reading upside-down, I could make out two words, 'Police Sergeant', so I guessed at least one of the reasons why I was here. I sat back in my chair, looking him straight in the eye.

"Jim Boy," he said, tapping the paper in front of him and then reading out the contents, "what have you got to say to that?"

"Well, Colonel Sir, it's like this, these English bobbies have got it in for me. For one thing, I look after your car and they are jealous of me, and I never said I was your mate, either. They do their best to make me look bad all the time, and they don't like it because I clean your car and like GIs!"

The Colonel sat there, not even blinking. I was doing my best to alienate him against them, saying they said they didn't like the U.S. Army, and so on!

The Colonel interrupted, pointed out one finger at me and said:"You are a regular gas-ass by all accounts!"

I had no answer to that, so I just nodded!

"Look, Jim Boy, I'll tell you what I'll do. If you can keep out of trouble of any kind for one month from today – I'll make a note of today's date," he mumbled to himself, and jotted down notes in his large diary – "now, if you can stay clean for one month, I'll give you an authorisation, signed personally by myself, that you can drive any vehicle in the confines of this here Depot, and," he added, pointing his finger at me, "just get your arse tangled up again and you are fired! Is that crystal clear, Jim Boy?"

"Yes, Colonel Sir," I fired back at him, "just watch me, I'll stay out of trouble!"

"You're darn right, I'll watch you!" he said, and his gaze moved to the packages of cigars and Bull Durham cigarette tobacco and papers on his desk, which I had brought along with me.

"Say, does your old man let you smoke?"

"Well," I replied, "not really."

"But – well, can you roll this Bull Durham tobacco?"

"No, Colonel Sir," I said, thinking even the bloody manufacturers couldn't roll it into cigarettes, that's why they left it to fools like us! It was just like lumpy sawdust, but after saying that, a fairly good smoke!

"You're darn right, I'll watch you!"

"Well, don't mention this to your Dad and I'll show you how we do it in the States!"

He took the Bull Durham pouch, pulled out a cigarette paper, and 'pouring' the powder-type tobacco along left and right until there was enough on the paper, pulled the string in the neck of the pouch tight with his teeth. He then commenced to roll the cigarette. On completion, he handed it to me. He then took the table lighter, gave me a light, and I puffed away!

"Howzat?" he said, sitting back in his chair beaming, "and don't tell your old man I showed you how to roll, okay? Now, on your way, and keep out of trouble!"

"Thanks, Colonel Sir," and I left the office.

I went down the stairs, along the corridor, and down the steps of HQ, feeling very buoyant and cocky! Taking big puffs from my fag, I crossed the road and started to make my way back to the Motor Pool section, when I heard a familiar voice in the distance shouting: "Jim, get that bloody cigarette out of your mouth or I'll stuff it down your throat!" It was Dad! I ran like hell in the opposite direction!

It now meant I was faced with an almost impossible task. To keep out of trouble for a month! However, I was determined to do just that, even if it meant me staying away from work!

I thought back to my dressing down by Colonel Richland. What a grand fellow he is. Fancy giving me, yes me, a real driving licence to drive anything! That meant anything from a bulldozer to a tank! Mind you, I had already done that, but it would be all legal and above board, and I'd show those bobbies in the Depot! But, first, let's get the licence and I'll drench the first bugger it see!

CHAPTER 18

My Buddy 'Father Kelly'

HOW in the hell could I possibly keep out of trouble? It meant that I would have to avoid all the opportunities that came my way nearly every minute of the working day!

I carried on washing and changing the oils on the staff cars, up to now I had found about eight 'french letters' in different vehicles (but not in the Colonel's car!) and I planned to get some special gas soon and inflate them and let them loose over the Depot when the dinner hooter went, and see what the reaction of all the office girls would be when they floated over their heads as they queued outside the canteen, but I thought I'd wait until I got my licence!

I heard a horn tooting at the front of the garage and there, in a jeep, was Technical Sergeant Fortio. He always reminded me of Mussolini, though I didn't tell him that!

"Say, Jim," he shouted over to me, "where in the hell is the Cletrac?"

Now a Cletrac was simply a rubber-tracked vehicle, nearly all engine up front, steered by the usual levers, and had things like an air-compressor on board, a large winch and numerous other extras, and was used a lot on U.S. airfields to tow aircraft and trailers loaded with bombs.

"I don't know!" I shouted back.

"Aw, shit, man! I gotta have that Cletrac, pronto!"

"Why's that?" I replied.

"Captain Ransome wants to pull his office outa the mud by the instrument shop and move up on to a dry piece of land. It ain't no good using a 6x6 (large truck). Even the goddam wrecker truck is bogged down too!"

What's wrong with getting a bloody Sherman from the Tank Shop?" I shouted back.

"I ain't got no tank drivers up there, for Christ sake, and, anyway, you can drive a Sherman, can't ya? I'll give you a carton of Chesterfields, son. Go and ask your old man, he'll give you the okay!"

"No chance, mate," I said, "he'll bloody kill me if I ask him, and Colonel Richland has had me up to his office and threatened to fire me if I as much look at a tank!"

Just then, the Cletrac came rumbling up the road and pulled to a halt outside dad's office. T/Sgt Fortio jumped out of his jeep and ran over and spoke to the driver.

"Say, buddy, can you pull Captain Ransome's office a few yards up the road on to dry ground?"

The driver looked down at the T/Sgt. "I'm just going for chow, and another thing, you gotta get a requisition from the Motor Pool Office!"

"OK, get a requisition!"

"Sorry," says the driver, "you gotta get that yourself."

"Aw, shit!" replied the T/Sgt, "just sit right there, I'll be right back," and off he went to the Motor Pool office.

I walked over to the Cletrac. The driver was from our 'pool' and his name was P. F. C. Sader. We called him Sadie, for short, which he didn't mind at all.

"How you doing, Sadie?"

"Not bad, Jimmy. What the hell's that creep needing a Cletrac to pull some office a few yards down the road, God knows. No wonder we ain't won the war yet! Them officers are more worried about getting their shiney shoes all muddy. Makes me sick!"

"Yeah, me too!" I replied.

Sadie was chewing on half on unlit cigar, occasionally spitting the juice on the hot muffler of the Cletrac, which made a loud sizzling noise.

"Yeah," he repeated again, "no wonder we ain't won the war yet!"

After a few minutes, T/Sgt Fortio came hurrying back, waving the authorisation. Handing it up to Sadie he said "Here y'are, son, follow me back and we'll get the darn job done in just a few minutes."

I thought it might be interesting to watch, So I hopped up alongside Sadie and off he roared, following the jeep to the instrument shop. We soon reached the office, which was really a large packing case made of wood, very large, about twenty feet by ten by eight high, on sort-of skids. It was surrounded by water, a few inches deep, with thick, slimey mud. Nearby was a Diamond T wrecker truck, bogged down to the axles, well and truly stuck!

As we surveyed the scene, Captain Ransome, with a cigar jammed between his teeth, opened the office door and shouted over to T/Sgt Fortio. "OK, let's get this show on the road!" and he waded out through the water and mud until he reached the firmer ground. It was now my dinner-break, but I thought I would give them a hand, and it seemed too good to miss!

"Say, Jimmy, pull this winch wire out and hook it onto the steel lifting eye on the end of the office," said T/Sgt Fortio.

I had no rubber boots on, so I stripped off my shoes and socks, rolled up my trouser leg, and took the steel winch wire across to the hooking eye and snapped it in. By this time, quite a large audience had assembled (well out of the way) and Sadie took the strain on the hawser from about fifty feet to try and pull the flood-bound office forward. Slowly, it inched forward as Sadie revved the motor on the Cletrac, then it stuck, refusing to budge.

By now Captain Ransome and Sgt Fortio were both shouting confusing instructions to Sadie, who called out "Aw, shit, Captain, this here thing ain't gonna pull that son-of-a-bitch out, you need a goddam Cat!"

"Just give it the gun, soldier!" T/Sgt Fortio shouted, and Sadie took up the strain again.

Everyone was standing ankle-deep in mud and water and, as the winch tightened up under the load, could see it slowly unwinding! Fortunately, Dad had forewarned me in the past about this happening, because it meant that, very quickly, the wire would break and if you didn't hit the deck you were minus a head or limb.

"Hit the deck, the wire's breaking!" I shouted as loud as I could, pointing to the wire.

Captain Ransome and T/Sgt Fortio had spotted it at the same time as I had and, together, we all hit the muddy water, face first, as it went *TWANG* and parted with a loud cracking sound, and whipped over the heads, just a few feet from the ground!

Sadie switched off his motor and jumped down and ran over to the Captain as he was stumbling to his feet. We all stood up, finally, covered all over the front in mud and slime!

The Captain was fuming and started to blame the T/Sgt who, in turn, started to blame Sadie, and I slowly walked backwards, pretending I was only a spectator, trying to disengage myself from the operation.

"You told me to give her the gun, Sarge!" cried Sadie. "I told you that you needed a Cat, now I gotta draw a new wire and fitting it is a hell-of-a-job!"

"Oh, shit on your wire, Sadie, just haul-ass out of it," shouts Sgt Fortio.

Just then, Dad walked round the corner.

"What the hell are you doing in that mess, Jim? What the devil are you poking your nose in up here?"

"Sadie asked me to give him a hand, Dad, and the winch-wire has snapped."

"Stupid sods!" Dad mumbled, and he walked over to where the Captain and Sergeant were trying to wipe the mess off their faces!

"Hello, Sir," Dad addressed the Captain, "looks like you're in trouble. Can I help you out?"

"You sure can Eddy," replied the Captain, "look at this lot here!"

Dad surveyed the office and eyed the broken wire. "I'll get Sgt Kelly down with the Caterpillar and sort it out. Where do you want the office, Captain?"

"Just pull it to hell out of there and leave it on the highway, and while you're at it, would you pull that Wrecker truck out as well?" The useless goddam thing!"

Dad went off back to the Motor Pool, calling me as he went, and giving me a rollicking as we walked down the road. I was covered in mud and soaking wet!

"Get those clothes off and get cleaned up, Jim," he was saying, "you can always be counted on to be where you're not supposed to be and, by the way, when you're cleaned up, come over to the office and you can come up with me and Sgt Kelly with the Cat, and I'll show you the right way to go about the job."

Dad was like that, he would shout first, but after he would show you how to do any job in the correct way.

When Sgt Kelly arrived with the Cat at the Motor Pool, I had cleaned up and had a bite to eat. Dad and I climbed up alongside Kelly and away we trundled to the Instrument Shop.

This Cat was a massive piece of machinery and to ride on it so high up on the driver's seat really gave me a thrill, but the vibration on the hard road made your eyes wobble in their sockets.

Kelly was some driver. He was another guy who never lit his cigar, but just chewed on the end and, with practised precision, could spit the brown juice at any particular spot, usually on my head if I teased him!

"Here," shouted Dad over the roar of the giant motor, "swing your back-end round there and back up just in front of the office, and Jim, you stay where you are and watch what we do!"

Kelly swung this way and that, then backed up as instructed and stopped, then jumped down and connected a heavy chain from the back tow-bar onto the eye-hook on the office. Dad stood back, now armed with Wellington boots he was squelching around, giving orders. He told Kelly to "take it away," which he did and, slowly but surely, he pulled the office right out and up on to the highway and then unhitched the chain. The Captain and T/Sgt Fortio clapped their hands and thanked Dad for his help. Dad nodded and just added, casually, "if you use the right tool for the right job, it very rarely fails!"

I returned to the Motor Pool on the Cat with Sgt 'Father' Kelly. I liked him very much. He was nicknamed 'Father' by the guys in his company because he was a very religious man and a very strange one too! He worked like a slave all through the week, but no way would he miss his Sunday morning mass. He would spruce up in his best uniform and, come rain or shine, he would go to church! There was a little RC church, only a hut, in Ludgershall. But, here is where he differed a little from his buddies. After the service he would start by going to the pubs, mostly he used the Crown in Ludgershall, getting tanked up with booze. He would drink until closing time, about 2 p.m. and, loaded with extras, he would sneak back into base and drink for the rest of the day at the billets.

Many a time I would call up at the barracks on a Sunday afternoon and there he was, drinking merrily away, but he would never take a drink with anyone. Then he would pile his drinks on the top bunk and, with every glass he drank, the more ridiculous his behaviour became. He would go on and on!

"I toast Adolf Hitler and all his goddam Nazis for starting this war," – he would go on – "That's how I'm a buck sergeant, because there's a war on, see, and because I'm a buck sergeant I'm in charge of a bunch of greenhorns and have to take orders from chicken-shit lieutenants and captains and colonels," and, raising his glass again, he'd say, "Here's to all them goddam useless brass-hats."

While all this was going on, no-one would say a word or protest. It was best to ignore him, but sometimes tempers frayed. 'Father' Kelly would go on and on until about six o'clock then, finally, fall asleep but, until then, usually, no-one would tell him to shut-up because, if they did, he would start preaching the gospel and would not stop, so the few occupants of the billets who were unfortunate not to have a pass or were confined to barracks, from past experience, would let him ramble on. So he would go on and on . . . until tempers flared.

"Why are you GIs here? I'll tell you why, because you were told to come here, that's why! Like sheep to the slaughter, and why didn't you refuse to come? Because you're chicken-shit, the whole goddam lot of you! That's why I'm here, I'm chicken-shit too! But I admit it see!"

He'd take another gulp from his bottle, then, pointing to me with bleary eyes he'd say "See that Limey kid over there? He's the only one here out of the whole goddam bunch of you who's not chicken-shit! Why? Because he never refused to come over here. Why's that? Because he was already here, he had no choice see?" and he would burst out into hysterical laughter. "He was here when the goddam war started – he! he! – him and thousand of other Limeys, and they've been fighting this war on their own while we've been sitting back home on our arses, they've been going through hell on earth, when we should have been over here!" Then lifting his bottle to his lips again, he'd say "Here's to the Limeys . . ." as he spilled some beer down his shirt!

"Aw, shut your mouth, Kelly, for Christ's sake, I'm trying to sleep," came a voice from down the bottom of the hut, obviously tired of Kelly's tirade. Turning his head, Kelly looked flabbergasted at the interruption.

"You tell me to shut my mouth, you goddam chicken-shit rebel! Don't you know God so loved the world that he gave his only begotten son, that whosoever believeth in him would not perish on Perham Down but live an everlasting life, see!"

"What the hell's that got to do with this goddam war?" shouted back the rebel.

"I'll tell you what it's got to do with this war. It's 'cause you have to believe in something, like f'rinstance, you think the Germans ain't got no right to start a war and invade and kill thousands of innocent people. So you take a side on the righteous, because you believe so much in liberty, freedom, and all that shit! So you gotta go and fight them Japs and them Krauts. So you may have to lay down your goddam life for some useless goddam people, but you do that, because you love them, you see? And you believe in democracy and freedom, follow me?'

"Don't talk crap, Kelly!" came an unknown voice from the end of the billet, "I don't love no-one that much, specially someone I don't now. I ain't fighting for Roosevelt or that bunch up in the White House, or the Stars and Stripes, or that 'Liberty' shit, see! I fight for myself and make sure as hell I get back to the damn slum I was brought up in, with my Ma taking in washing and working herself to death, yeah! You talk about all this laying down your life for those you love. Ha! You're drunk, Kelly, just drunk, and tomorrow you'll be sober, back to work, working your balls off, for what, and who? This war ain't gonna change anything! No, nothing! Sure, we'll win 'cause we are better than them Japs and Krauts. So what? Beating them ain't winning! After we smash up their goddam cities and towns, then what? After the war we gotta feed 'em, give them money to rebuild their damn countries, so in another twenty or thirty years they come back and give us another kick up the fanny! While back in the States, if we ever get back there, we go on at the same old pace, no changes, plenty of promises and all that crap from the politicians about – vote for me and him and the other guy – but, let me tell you, Kelly, when, and if, you get back home, you try preaching that to some guy who's had his balls blown off, or is blind as a bat, when they go looking for a job, or a decent pension! Kelly, you're full of shit, you're a hypocrite! You get pissed-up on Sunday, after going to church, and come back here and start all this 'love' crap. Let me tell you, Kelly, I love me! Next comes my pay call, and last of all, when I get in my bunk I don't want to hear any of your preaching about fighting for liberty. The losers in this war will be the winners. So shut your goddam holy trap!"

Kelly took another swig and, after a thoughtful pause, replied, "You just don't like Sergeants, that's your trouble. You don't like nothin' but your own shiny ass! Me, I get drunk, sure, but I got principles, see? I believe in all that freedom and liberty, and I believe in God! More so, I believe in the good old United States and all of them people who don't want no Japs or Krauts walking all over their faces. So, here's to all those who love one another and love liberty and freedom!" With that, 'Father Kelly' slumped down in his bunk and peace and quiet returned once again – till the following Sunday!

On Monday I started work at the Depot at 8.00 a.m. and, usually, the first person I would meet would be 'Father Kelly'. He would stroll in with his eyes on his cheeks, slowly recovering from his usual Sunday booze-up.

"Hi, Jim."

"Hi, Kelly," I replied. "Christ, you look bad, Kelly!"

"Not half as bad as I feel!" he groaned.

"Why do you drink so much, Kelly? Surely you could drink in moderation and save a few bucks, or send a bit extra back home to your family."

"Ain't got no family back home, Jim!"

"You gotta have someone somewhere, Kell, somewhere you hang your hat!"

"No, I ain't go no-one."

Kelly started to check the oil levels on his massive Caterpillar. Today he would be driving the Cat with a crane boom fitted and he would, meticulously, go over his machine, whichever model he would be using on that particular day, every morning, first thing.

Kelly was a man of about thirty years of age, with a broken nose, stocky build, quiet when he was at work, and an extremely hard worker. He would get his grease-gun and grease each of the large track rollers, then he would fill the gasoline tank on the 'donkey engine' (a small engine which was used to swing over the main diesel engine), then fill up the main diesel tank and check things over generally.

"You mean to say that when you go back home you got no-one to go back to, Kell?" I heaved myself up and sat on the massive track.

"That sure is true, Jim, and anyhow I might not get back home, might I? There's a war on, remember, and some of us will go back home and some won't. Got to accept that, you know, Jim!" Kelly was humming to himself and I stood there watching him.

"What a strange attitude to take, Kell. You got to reach for the sky, you know, and everyone's got to believe that they will be the lucky ones, don't you agree, Kell?"

"No, luck, ain't got nothin' to do with it, son. It's fate, that's what it is."

"Why do you work hard all week and then get pissed-up on Sundays, Kell? I mean, it's got no point, has it?" I said, lighting a fag and trying to look serious. Kelly looked hard at me, still tinkering about, servicing his machine.

"D'ya know, Jim, for a little guy you sure do ask a lot of big questions!" he stated, plainly trying to avoid giving me a straight answer, "but I'll try and tell you why. One reason is that I have been a loner. I've driven these all my working life," he said, tapping the track of his Cat, "and sitting up there all day, year in and out, you get kinda detached. I do, anyway, and I was left on my own when I was only fourteen years old, and had to shine shoes, wash dishes, serve gas, sell papers, anything to make a few bucks. I ended up one day working on a new turnpike and very soon I was getting some practice on these Cats and different earth-moving machines, and I'd work like a bastard for six days a week, then on a Sunday morning I'd go to mass and then go on the beer all day. That was my life then, is now, and even though I'm in the army, I ain't changed none since. These here machines are my life, really, I ain't known nothin' different. Pass me up that oil can, Jim! Yeah, that's it, son, now you know!"

"So you'll go back after the war and carry on where you left off?" I said.

"Well, I never really left off, did I? but yes, I guess you could say that, Jim. If I get back! Better start this baby," he said and he started up the donkey engine, then pulled in the two levers and started the main engine with a loud roar, a cloud of smoke belching out of the large exhaust.

I waved to Kelly and he shoved his machine in gear and moved off down the road to the railway sidings, where he would be working like a dog all day, with a cloud of dust in his wake.

I went back to the Motor Pool office. Dad was busy handing out all the trip tickets to the GI drivers who would be taking all kinds of war supplies to different parts of the country.

"Here you are, Jim," Dad shouted, "go with this driver on the White tractor and Fruehauf trailer to Southampton and drop off the load and get back as quick as you can, we're short of trucks, so you go with P. F. C. Jenkins and show him the way. Make sure he doesn't get lost, as it's his first trip out, and here's your subsistence money, so get moving!

He introduced me to P. F. C. Jenkins, who was a negro of very short stature, with big, staring eyes. We climbed up into the large tractor unit. Some tractor this! Built by White in the U.S. It was fitted with a large cab and Westinghouse air brakes. It had a fifth wheel on top of the rear axles and pulled a large, flat, or box van trailer.

"What's your first name, mate?" I said to me driver, who was getting ready to start the engine.

"Jus' call me Justin," he replied, with a huge grin flashing nearly a whole mouthful of gold teeth! Christ, I thought, he must have the whole Federal gold reserve in there!

Justin started the engine and soon we were out on the main road to Southampton, thirty miles away. He was, by modest description, a gas-ass (an American expression for a crazy, fast driver) and in no time was thundering along at fifty miles per hour, and wandering from one side of the road to the other.

"Hey, Justin, slow down mate and keep over on the left-hand side of the road, you're not in the States you know, slow down and drive at no more than 40 mph."

"Don't panic, man! Jus' let J.J. get you there all in one piece, 'cos I'm the best driver south of the Mason-Dixon Line!"

"Yeah, I know," I replied, as we approached a long, steep hill, and, thankfully, the White, with its heavy load, started to slow down and labour up the long climb.

"Yeah, man, I used to haul up from Memphis to Knoxville. Regular trips they were. Used to have some fun, sonny boy."

"OK," I said, "keep your eyes on the road J.J. and, by the way, let's see the documents on the load description."

I reached over to the sheaf of papers clipped to the dashboard and leafed through them.

"Christ Almighty! Sixteen tons of hand-grenades!"

"Shit, man!" J.J. shouted, "what you say, man? Hand-grenades?" and with that, he pulled up, gingerly, over on the grass verge and stopped. "Let's get down, man," he said, "and check that the goddam load ain't shifted none! No-one says nothin' to me about no grenades!"

We walked round to the back of the large Fruehauf van trailer and released the clasps on the doors. We were parked up in a country road near Stockbridge by a disused lime-processing plant and I climbed up into the back, checked the cases, all were packed neatly and had not moved.

"Here, jump up J.J. and check yourself."

"You gotta be kidding man. I ain't getting tangled up with no grenades. They're bad news, man. Jus' the sight of them makes me shit ma self!"

"Don't be daft, J.J. they ain't primed, they can't be, Dad would have told me!"

"Tell you they were primed? He didn't even tell you they were on the goddam truck? Your Dad don't give a shit about you – or me!"

"Look, J.J. are you a betting man?"

J.J. looked at me and I could see a look of suspicion clouding his face as he wiped his hands up and down his tunic nervously. "One thing is sure, son, I don't make no bets within a mile of these mean-looking babies!"

"OK," I replied, "I say they ain't primed see, and I'll tell you what, I'll open a case and we'll have a look. I've had instruction on grenades in the army cadet force," I lied, "and I know just by looking at one if they are hot grenades or not!"

"Look, sonny boy, I'd feel a lot better if I knew if they were safe, meanwhile, I'll go and take a leak and you make a quick check."

J.J. made a hasty retreat and I quickly started to open the grenade case and, after a lot of difficulty, pulled the lid off. Wow! the case was full of the deadly things! I picked one up and could see right away that it was ready for action.

I could feel my scalp tingling with excitement. Here's a chance to let one off out here where it's quiet, I thought. I put two, carefully, into my pocket and climbed down off the trailer as J.J. came back through the bushes, buttoning his flies up.

"Well, sonny," he beamed, "what's the low down? Are they live or not?"

"Yes, they are live!" I replied, as I took one out of my pocket and went to hand it to him.

J.J. froze for a moment, then went berserk and backed up smartly with outstretched arms.

"Don't pull that pin, man, we's all goin' to glory if ya does, and I don't want no glory for a long time yet!"

"Don't worry, J.J. I ain't stupid!"

"Stupid!" he shouted, his voice shaking, "you're goddam crazy, that's all! Put that son-of-a-bitch back in the case and let's get to Southampton and drop that goddam trailer off!"

I put my hand in my other pocket and pulled out the other grenade and tossed them up together, making sure I caught them!

"Christ! You are crazy, man," screamed J.J. and ran back down the road a few yards and jumped into the ditch. He then peeped his head out and shouted "I'll tell your Pa, he'll sure as hell kill you if you don't kill us both first! I heard some tales about you in the billets and they're all true! Now I ain't gonna get up in that tractor till you put them back safely and lock them doors! So, please yourself, man."

"Look, J.J., keep your head down and I'll throw one in the quarry, it won't hurt you none if you keep your head well down! Just pretend we're throwing one at the Krauts!"

I put one grenade back in my pocket and put one finger through the ring on the pin and made sure I held the grenade tight in the palm of my hand, making sure the release lever was clasped tight.

J.J. was shouting still, "Don't pull that pin, you'll blow our asses up like confetti! I promised my Ma I'd come back home, balls and all!"

Laughing, I withdrew the pin and, with all my strength, threw the grenade into the empty lime quarry and fell flat on my face, shouting to J.J. to keep his hand on his halfpenny and, with an almighty roar the grenade exploded, bringing a large shock wave and all kinds of chalk and rubbish on top of me and the trailer. I looked around and saw J.J. pop his head up from the ditch down the road, his large eyes bolting out of his head! I got to my feet and ran up to him.

"Come on!" I shouted, "you throw the other one J.J. it won't harm you. If you don't know how to use these, how the hell you going to look after yourself if your life depends on it, eh?"

J.J. was now plucking up courage, not wanting me to see him chicken.

"It ain't that," he shouted, "that would have waked up all the goddam MPs in the place and, anyway, I'm in the ordnance not the infantry. No, sir! I ain't touching one of them babies!"

White dust was settling everywhere and as we had been stopped for fifteen minutes or so, I thought we had better move on.

"OK, J.J. I'll put the other one back in the case and let's get moving, and we'll hightail it out of here!"

I jumped up in the trailer and put the grenade back in the case and soon we were humming down the road once more.

J.J. was very quiet now. He kept glancing across at me say, "You are crazy, man, I sure as hell won't like falling out with you. I can't wait to drop this trailer and get back to the Depot tonight!"

We pulled into the docks at Southampton at last. It was about lunch time and, after we had dropped our trailer, we were instructed to hook up another trailer loaded with synthetic rubber for tyre re-treading to go to Tidworth, as, during one part of the war, tyres were in very short supply and the U.S. Army had to resort to re-treading.

After having some 'chow' we made our way back to Tidworth. J.J. drove very carefully, following my instructions to the letter on speed and warnings of dangerous bends or bridges ahead of us. I felt sorry for him. He didn't belong in this war, but then, who did? Guys like J.J. were compelled to go to war. They came from all walks of life. There were just a few Al Capone types that cross my path, but there is no room in my memory for them.

It was almost teatime as we pulled into the Motor Pool at the Depot and Dad came out of the office and called me over to where he was standing. His face was white as a sheet and I knew by his expression that something was very seriously wrong. He took me to one side.

"Look, son, I have some bad news for you, so brace yourself!"

"What is it, Dad? Is Mum ill?"

"No, son, she's okay. It's Father Kelly, I'm afraid, he had an accident with his Cat this morning, and he's dead!"

I could feel the tears welling up in my eyes. Oh, my God, I thought, it can't be true! Dad put his arm round my shoulders and led me back to the office.

"Come on, son, I'll get you a cup of tea."

I sat down in Dad's office trying to sip the cup of tea he gave me. I couldn't hold back my tears. My hand shook and I had to put my tea down on the table.

"It's all right, son, don't be ashamed of crying. I've seen grown men crying. It's a kind of safety valve, you see. I know you and Father Kelly were good mates. He once told me you were the only true friend he ever had, and you will find in war, and in peace, we all have to lose someone we are fond of, or someone we love, it's all part of our lives. Good news, good times, bad times, mostly bad times, Jim. When this war is over we'll get a little garage somewhere local and everything will work out okay, and some day you will look back on all this as experience."

I sat there silent. Nothing in this world right now, or any other time it seemed, could bring Father Kelly back or any of my other friends who had died. How many more of my buddies would I have to lose by the time peace was made again? If it ever did come! It was many days before I was anything like myself again, but I never really did get over the death of such a good friend.

97

I never knew the full details of how he died, but I believe he was crushed between the front of the armoured shield of his Cat and a large packing case he had been lifting jointly with another Cat off a railway wagon. Apparently, the crate jammed and he broke a strict rule by leaving his seat while his crane was taking the strain on the jib. Maybe the case slid back and crushed him. I believe that's what happened.

Kelly had been an excellent friend to me. The chats we had together. He used to read me a few verses from the Bible, a small one which he always carried in his left breast pocked.

So many heartfelt thanks, Father Kelly, for the time you bothered to take out of your short, hard life to pass on to me some good advice and some words of wisdom from your little Holy Bible. For all your many good deeds and, despite your sins, I know you have a well-deserved place in heaven.

CHAPTER 19

In The Hot Seat!

S O it went on. Every day presented a different scene and new challenge! It was always exciting, every minute of every day. The GIs were good to work with and were always ready to show me how to operate various kinds of military equipment. That is, probably, the reason why I could understand the operation of so many vehicles!

After work, at around 5.45 p.m., Dad would drive me home with some of his friends from the Depot, in the Clement Talbot or, sometimes, I would get a lift from one of the friendly GIs in one of the staff cars.

Soon, the day arrived when a phone call came from HQ that Colonel Richland wanted to see me and, as a month had passed since he promised me a licence to drive if I kept out of trouble in the Depot, I knew what he wanted me for!

I arrived, as arranged, at 3.00 p.m. at the Colonel's office. As usual, Eileen admitted me and asked me to sit down and wait a few minutes in the Colonel's office, as he would return in a few minutes.

I sat down opposite his large desk. I gazed over to his large, swivelled, armchair and out of the window, from which he could view the coming and going of everyone through the main gate and the main thoroughfare. On the wall were various maps and one very large map of England, with different markings dotted here and there. I looked around, quickly, and wondered if there was time to take a quick squat in his chair before he returned! I edged around the large polished desk and, as everything sounded quiet, except for the distant tap-tap of a typewriter, I pulled out the chair a few inches and sat down!

Suddenly, I felt like the God of Tidworth Depot! I felt transformed! I leaned back and swung gently from side to side, pretending I had an audience of top brass and was giving them instructions on how best to run the place. I nodded to one side and shook my head to the other, as the imaginary audience sat making suggestions, which I either like or disliked. I opened the lid on a cigarette box. No! I had better not light up, I haven't got my licence yet!

I swung right around on the chair, facing the window. What a view he had of the whole of Tidworth, and beyond! I thought I could feel the power of the chair coming up through my backside. All I gotta do is pick up the phone and say to everyone, "This is Colonel Richland, I'm stopping the war for one day, you can all go home!" Or ring up the canteen and order a crate of Coke and a carton of fags, or tell the civilian Depot Police Chief to get stuffed and leave Jim Stoodley to do as he wants, because I'm the big wheel round here, get me!

I was transformed, very promptly, back to Jim Stoodley by the office door opening, and who should step in but Colonel Richland himself. I, instinctively, jumped up out of his chair and opened my mouth, but nothing came out!

"May I come in?" said the Colonel, half smiling to himself. "No, sit down, I'll sit here, seeing as you seem to prefer that one! Okay, Jim, make yourself comfortable. Now, about this authorisation to drive . . ." He leaned across the desk. "Excuse me, 'Colonel'," he joked, "just let me get that basket," and he drew the basket over to his side and pulled out a slip of paper and read its contents to me:

> To whom it may concern.
> This is an authority for the bearer, James A. Stoodley, to drive any type of vehicle in the confines of the Tidworth Ordnance Depot.

It was signed, and dated by the Colonel himself.

He sat there, holding the piece of paper in his hand, looking intensely at me. I can see him now, his large frame sitting on that small chair opposite me, pretending, for the moment, that I was the Colonel. That this man, with his position and responsibility, could fine a little time to let me play the part, and in his chair, spells out his great character!

"How does it feel to be the big wheel, sonny?"

I opened my mouth but, again, nothing came out!

"Speechless are you, Jim? Now, see, that's how I am when I'm snowed under with work every day, and some guy phones me up and starts complaining about Jim Stoodley doing this or that, which he's not supposed to be at! Well, seeing that you have kept your nose clean, that I know of, I am giving you this here licence as promised, in the hope that it will help win the war and not lose it. Okay?"

"Yes, Sir!" I managed to get out at last, "I do appreciate that more than you will ever know. I think you're the most considerate man I've ever met!"

"I know I am!" replied the Colonel, I could see him smiling to himself, "and I must be the craziest too! So don't try to hand me no bullshit, see!"

"I wouldn't try to do that, Colonel Richland. I respect you far too much for that!"

"Yeah! Yeah! Okay, Jim," said the Colonel, getting out of the chair, "just remember I was your age once. I've been through it all myself. If you let me down again, I'll get shipped back to the States, that's for sure!"

He gave me the licence and I got out of his chair, making sure I pushed it back tidy. I folded the licence, carefully, my heart skipping a beat. He saw me to me office door and pointed a finger at me.

"Don't forget, Jim, driving only in the Depot. Okay? Just put your nose outa them main gates in a truck or anything else and you're in the stockade! Now, on your way and prove my trust in you!"

"Right, Sir, I will," I replied, "Cheerio, Sir, thanks again!"

"Oh, by the way, Jim, you ain't been anywhere near that airfield have you?"

"Oh, no Sir!"

"Good!" and he closed the door behind me.

I walked through Eileen's office, waving to her as I went. She smiled back and said "Good luck," then I was gone!

CHAPTER 20

Tech. Sergeant Abe Schlamn

TODAY promised to be a glorious one, even at 8.00 a.m. on this summer's morning one could feel the heat in the light breeze that rolled over Salisbury Plain. I was in the park outside the tank repair shop; today I would be riding out in an M5 light tank, as passenger, on a trial run over the testing area, with a Technical Sergeant named Abe Schlamn. There was a lot of activity all round the park, motors revving up, smoke hung lazily in the air. I had a great feeling of excitement about me; how lucky I was, I thought, being able to enjoy such adventures and especially with these GIs who seemed such a world apart from my own countrymen.

I could see Abe coming over to where I was standing. He was wearing fatigues and carried a clipboard under his arm. I studied him as he made his way over to me, dark-skinned, average height, very dark, curly, hair. Age? Maybe 25 years old. I had known Abe for some time, as he was one of the test drivers for all tracked vehicles.

"Hi, Jim!" he shouted as he walked up, "you coming with me on this trip, aren't you?"

"Yes, Abe," I replied, "nice day for it ain'it it?"

"Sure is, buddy. Here, have a Camel," he replied, handing me a smoke.

"Thanks, Abe."

"Now, let's see, Jim, we're going to take an M5, yeah? We'll particularly give the automatic transmission a good test, and also check for propshaft vibration. In other words, we'll have a nice three hours in the countryside. Suit you, son?"

"Yes!" I replied, "that's great, and can I take over the dual driving controls when we get out on the course?"

"Sure, Jim, so let's look for this M5, eh?" We walked down the line of tanks, Abe looking for the registration number as we went.

"Here she is, Jim!" he exclaimed. There was a name stencilled on the side of it in bold capitals: *King Solomon*! We climbed aboard, Abe taking the driver's seat and myself sitting alongside him in the co-driver/machine-gunner's position. Abe called over: "Put your helmet on, Jim, and here, give this trip ticket to he MPs on the gate as we go out!"

"Okay, Abe," I replied, and he started up the two Cadillac engines. I could feel the blood pounding in my temples, I was so excited! We moved off down towards the main gate. I passed the trip ticket to the MP and away we went, off to the testing ground, five miles out in the hills. One could feel the surge of power as we gathered speed, the breeze blowing into our faces, kissing our cheeks with its warmth. I strapped on my throat microphone and plugged in the headphones and, soon, we were turning off the main road onto the track which would lead us to the test area.

Abe passed me a bar of candy and proceeded to carry out the tests. The steering levers on the M5 were fixed from above and one had to reach up both arms to steer, a little tiresome after a while! The going was getting pretty tough by now, we had slowed down to a mere crawl, the autobox changing smoothly up and down, through the gears, as required. Abe pulled up on a crest after fifteen minutes and signalled me we would climb down for a break.

"Yeah, I guess that gearbox feels okay, Jim, next we'll give that propeller shaft (main driving shaft) a real test by doing some steep climbs." We sat down on the warm turf.

"Oh boy, what a swell day, Jim," said Abe, as we lit our cigarettes.

"Where you from, Abe?" I asked.

"Me? From Brooklyn. My Pa brought me over from Germany a few years ago. He was a tailor, but died just before Pearl Harbor. My Ma, she died in Germany. I guess I was only three years old then."

"Gosh, I'm sorry to hear that, Abe!"

"Yeah! I guess I never remembered her, Jim. We couldn't stay in Germany, things were getting hard for us there, being Jewish. My dad had a hard time, so one day he said to me: 'Abe, we're going to what I've heard say is God's country.' So, me thinking that was Palestine, got quite a surprise when our ship berthed in New York. I remember seeing that Statue of Liberty as we sailed in. Gosh, that was something to remember, Jim!"

"I'd love to see that myself, Abe!" I replied.

"Yes, you gotta see that sight, Jim, it's really breathtaking. Me? After dad died, I used to alter clothes in a men's store. Joined the army in 1940. I could see us eventually getting into this lot, so I thought I'd fight for Uncle Sam or perhaps I really wanted to get back at Hitler in my own way. The things that guy has done to our people out there, Jim! People outside Germany haven't got any idea what he's doing. He's got to be stopped, and I guess that's what we're going to do. I'd love to meet that son-of-a-bitch face to face. Who knows, maybe I'll have the pleasure!"

103

"I hope you do, Abe," I replied. "I'd like to run over him with that M5 there, back and forth!" Abe laughed!

"You're mean, man! Real mean!"

"No," I replied, "that's only after you have cut his balls off!" Abe burst out with roaring laughter again.

"Gee whiz, Jim, you sure are some character!" Then, looking at his watch he said, "Well, Jim, I guess we'll get on and finish the tests and high-tail it back for chow! I should have brought some rations but, never mind, let's go now and we'll soon be back at the Depot."

We mounted up and set off to the steep parts of the course. This climbing frightened me a bit, because it seemed sometimes that the tank would rear up and fall on its back.

We had come to the really steep part of the climb now and the noise from the motor was deafening. We reached the summit and started, at full speed, down the other side. Down we went, faster still, now nearly at the bottom and touching 40 mph, when, suddenly, there was a terrible crunching sound, and out of the corner of my left eye, I saw the driveshaft come adrift from the front end between us and strike Abe under his right armpit! He let out a scream and fell forward.

I quickly grabbed the controls and, after a few moments, managed to stop the motion of the tank.

I climbed over to Abe. His body was limp and blood was spattered all over the white-painted interior. I eased him back in his seat. A trickle of blood was running down from his mouth, his right arm was lying limply down by his side, smashed! God! I thought, poor Abe. What am I going to do? The nearest help was miles back. I've got to do something quick, I thought, I looked at him again, he was mumbling something.

"What are you saying, Abe?" I shouted. I listened to his near unintelligible words.

"Drive me back to the Depot – quick – Jim . . . get me help . . . please . . ." he moaned.

"Don't worry, Abe, I'll get you there fast!"

I calculated I had about five miles to get him to Tidworth Military Hospital. God, help me get him there in time! Then it dawned on me, the tank was immovable – no shaft – I would have to run to the main road faster than I had ever run before! I looked quickly at Abe, tears flooding my eyes.

"Abe," I cried, "I've got to run for help. The tank's useless – hold on, buddy, you've got a war to win, remember?" And I was gone!

I flew like the wind, now my training would pay dividends! I took the short route to the road and, shortly, I staggered upon the main road. Luckily, it was always busy with U.S. Army traffic. I started to flag down trucks. Several wouldn't stop, then a command car pulled up on the other side. A captain, sitting alongside the driver, shouted over: "In trouble, sonny?"

I ran over to him, unable to speak, gasping for breath!

"Captain . . . my friend . . . Abe . . . the driver . . . badly hurt . . . we were out testing the tank and he's out there, very bad . . . hurt . . . please let me show you the way . . ."

"Here, son! Jump in! Show us where! Step on it, driver! Move! Move, man!" The driver turned the command car around, swiftly, and we raced off. Soon we were heading up towards the spot where Abe was waiting, desperately, for help!

"Around one more bend – over there, Captain – in that M5!"

"All-right, son, we'll soon get him to the infirmary!"

We arrived at the scene but getting poor Abe out of that confined space was murder. He was still groaning as we laid him along the back seat of the command car, and away we went over those terrifying bumps, shaking more pain through poor Abe's body!

We rejoined the main road at last and soon we arrived at the hospital. A stretcher was wheeled out and they took Abe inside. I went into the reception and gave the medics the details of the accident. I saw there for three hours, waiting for some news. Would he make it, I kept asking myself! He's got to, all his Mum and Dad went through under the Nazis, he's got to have a chance to get even himself! Then the doors swung open and over to me came the medic.

"You brought T/Sgt Schlamn in?"

"Yes," I replied. He saw down at my side, his face was very grim.

"Sgt Schlamn has had massive blood transfusions. His right arm has severe fractures and he has several broken ribs. I must be quite frank with you, he may not make it, but I'll say this, your prompt action may have possibly saved his life! All we can do is wait. If you would like to call up at 11.00 a.m. tomorrow we may be in a position to give you some positive news, either way! Okay?"

"Yes," I replied, "I'll call tomorrow," and made my way out of the hospital.

The next morning, I was back there again, promptly at 11.00 a.m.! The same medic came out.

"Come down and see him. He's a lot better today. You can just have five minutes with him. Okay? Do you feel better?"

"Sure do," I replied with delight.

"He's got you to thank for getting him here quickly. Only a few minutes later and he would certainly have died! Here, go in that door. You will see him, first bed on the left. Please be as quiet as you can."

I walked through the door and saw Abe lying in his bed, his eyes were closed and he was heavily swathed in bandages, I walked up to his bed and sat down on the chair beside him.

"Abe, Abe. It's me, Jim! Are you awake? It's me, Jim! I whispered. Abe opened his eyes, slowly, and seemed to recognise me. His breathing seemed laboured as he spoke: "Hi, Jim, nice of you to come."

"It's nice to see you, Abe," I replied. "Are you sure you feel well enough to see me?"

"Sure, Jim. I'm so glad you've come. I want to thank you for getting me here quickly, as the Doc says I lost so much blood that if I had not had transfusions right away, I guess I would have been a goner, and it's all thanks to you, Jim!" Abe paused for a moment, seemingly finding it hard to get his breath.

"Take it easy, Abe," I said, "just rest as much as you can. We all want you back back in the Depot." Abe tried to shift his position a little and tried to smile.

"I guess I won't be doing any more soldiering, Jim! The Doc says I have to go back to the States as soon as I'm bit better. My arm is all busted up and I have a lot of injuries to my chest too, so I guess we will have to forget that one, Jim!"

I looked at him lying there, all smashed up, thinking he sure has had his future ruined, another casualty of this war! When is all this suffering going to end, I wondered?

"Look, Abe," I said, "can I write a letter for you? You know, some relation you want me to drop a few lines to?"

"Ain't got none, Jim," Abe replied, "Ain't got no one, buddy!"

"Well, look, Abe, I'll come in and see you in a couple of days. Perhaps you will feel better, and don't let things get you down. When you're recovered in a few weeks, you can write to me and tell me how things are going for you! Just think, Abe, you will be enjoying all that lovely weather State-side.

"I reckon so, Jim, but I would sooner be over here fighting this war. Guess I ain't going to be much good to Uncle Sam, am I?" I could see Abe was getting a bit upset, so I made ready to leave.

"Look, Abe, I'll see you soon. Just get well, so-long pal!"

"See you soon, Jim," he replied, as I walked out through the door.

When I returned to the hospital a couple of days later, they told me that Abe had already gone to the States that morning, and the sister in charge handed over an envelope addressed to me. It was from Abe and he had got a nurse to write it down for him. I opened it, eagerly, and sat down in the waiting room to read it:

"Dear Friend Jim,
    It is very hard for me to write this letter to you, as I wanted to say goodbye and thank you, personally. As you now know as you read this letter, I had to leave here and I want to say thankyou for giving me such moral support and encouragement. There is no question about it, that you saved my life through your quick-thinking and getting me to the infirmary. There will never be a day that passes in my life without me thinking of you. I am so proud, and privileged to have had the honour to have you as a true friend. I hope that when this war is over we can meet again. Goodbye and God bless you. Most sincerely, Abe."

I walked out of the hospital, clutching his letter. I felt I would treasure it for the rest of my life. It made me feel as if I had done something worthwhile in my life for once.

I made my way back to work at the Depot and went up to Dad's office. He looked up as I walked in.

"How's Sgt Schlamn today, Jim?" Is he much better?" "He's gone back home. He's on his way now!"

"Where? To the States?"

"Yes, Dad, he left this note with the nurse to give to me. Here, you can read it, Dad," I said, handing it down to him.

Dad leaned back in his chair and opened the letter. He appeared to read it several times over then, without an upward glance, he folded the letter slowly and replaced it back into the envelope and held it up to me. I took it from his hand and, as I left without a word between us, I could see a tear roll down his cheek!

CHAPTER 21

The Shoot-Out On Windmill Hill!

IT was a beautiful morning, 6.00 a.m., and I had stayed all night in the hideout below ground in the plantation. I lit the primus stove, opened all the vents in the roof and rummaged in the larder for something really nice for breakfast. It was Sunday today and I could cook a few hot-dogs out of the tin, open a small tin of best butter, cut a few slices of U.S. Army bread, a little stale, but it would toast up lovely over the primus.

The smell of the hot-dogs hung against the low ceiling. Ah! This was the life! Plenty of good Wiltshire fresh air and loads of U.S. Army grub! Time to take the hot-dogs off and toast the bread. I lit up a Lucky Strike 'fag' and watched the smoke curl its way up and out of the vents. Ah! Toast done! On with the butter, really hard this stuff but the hot toast soon melts it down. I sit back against the chalk wall and get stuck in and think "What a war!" Crikey! I've forgotten the coffee! I'll open a K-ration where I know there is a tin of the best coffee, so it'll brew up while I'm eating breakfast. Christ! If the President could see me now, everything here was supplied by him! Yes, I'll drink a toast to him, way back there in the White House!

I looked at my Bulova wrist watch, 6.45 a.m. Good timekeeper this. I had it repaired in the instrument shop at the Depot for a GI friend of mine and, while it was being repaired, he had gone to the Stockade for ninety days for getting into trouble in the Bell public house at Weyhill, so I was wearing it proudly till he was released! It had a lovely blue crystal and, as I said, it was a perfect timekeeper and stood the recoil shocks from the sub-machine guns very well!

I started to think about what I might do today. Christ! I haven't got any toothpaste! I packed away all the cooking gear and went up top to have a good look around. The sun was coming up behind me through the clouds and there before me, stretching for miles, was the sweeping countryside I loved so much. Pity there was a war on really, but today it seemed all the world was at peace!

A slight breeze disturbed the pines around. It was warm on my cheek, soft it was, like a mother's kiss. I looked across the odd quarter-mile to the neighbouring pine tree plantation, and then to the others. No sign of

Jim in full combat gear on Salisbury Plain.

movement anywhere. It seemed to me that I was the only human up and about at this hour. I walked the few feet to the ammo and K-ration stock, which was so well concealed it was difficult to see it at all! There was plenty there, so I would take some food home later. I went back down the hideout for the binoculars and climbed a few feet up the small pine-tree and focused on the surrounding countryside. Not a sign of life anywhere, except a few birds and one or two rabbits hopping playfully out in the foreground.

Suddenly, I could hear all the air-raid sirens wailing like a dawn chorus. I could identify each one from each direction by the different pitches. Yes, that one is the Ludgershall siren way in the distance, and the other the one from Tidworth, not too far away. We expected air-raid alarms at any hour but it was a little unusual to have an alarm at this hour in the morning!

I'd better take the covers off the ·50 calibre machine-gun, I thought. I could feel my heart thumping in my ears as I ran up to the pit I had prepared months ago, uncovered the gun and ran back and picked up my GI helmet and, after a little delay, made the gun ready. I then dragged up two tin cases of spare ammo from my store, broke the inside tin waterproof seals for ready use. I wished I had John with me as, if I had to fire this gun, it would be hard work on my own. I pulled back the heavy cocking handle and then this baby was ready for any kind of trouble!

I then noticed a deathly silence had set it. Even the birds seemed to sense the danger. It was just like turning the radio off. Everything was quiet. I strained my ears for the tell-tale diesel-engined Gerry planes – nothing – but patience is a virtue. I'd sit and wait. Any low-flying, unsuspecting, enemy aircraft sneaking over my patch were going to get a stream of half-inch lead right up their 'jacksies' in quick time!

I sat back on the top of the sandbags, scanning the sky in all directions. I had a perfect all-round view and felt that I was ready as I ever would be! I'd better have a quick pee, I thought, no telling how long this alert would last!

Fifteen minutes had elapsed and, faintly, I could hear aircraft engines approaching! I grabbed the fist-grips on the fifty calibre and swung her round facing the direction I thought the sound was coming from, but out here on the plain, with trees scattered all over, it was deceiving as to where the right direction might be!

I glanced over my shoulder and there they were! Two Dorniers, flying pencils we called them, circling round towards my area, low, black and

Shoot-out on Windmill Hill.

menacing! There was no mistaking these buggers, one just knew they were Gerries. They just did not belong there, they meant bad business!

The leading plane was slightly lower than the other, sweeping wide and heading directly over my position. I lowered the gun barrel. This plane was low, damn it, I found I had set the tripod too high and I could not bring the barrel down low enough to bear on target!

The first plane flew straight over my head at zero feet, and on towards the direction of Tidworth, following the valley. As it passed over I could see a face peering down at me, in the nose, and the face wore a helmet. Then, with a deafening roar, it was over and gone!

I shifted my gaze to number two, coming up astern of him, quite some way back, but he was flying a bit higher and a little to my right. Boy! Is he in for a shock! My legs were shaking, uncontrollably, my palms were soaking wet, I could feel the sweat running down my ribs from under my armpits. I was shit-scared but, no matter, now's my chance, I'll blast this dirty sod! I felt as if the survival of England depended on me! On he came. I braced myself for the shock that would come when my thumbs

111

pressed the trigger. You didn't aim a fifty-calibre, you just pointed it in the general direction required!

I squeezed the trigger. The noise deafened me! I could see my tracers arcing out over the Dornier. I lowered the muzzle, but they were still over and now behind him. I swung further round to the right. My vision was blurred with the vibration from the gun, but now I put a stream of bullets ahead and saw the tracer glow of one or two of my bullets fly upwards after, seemingly, striking the front part of one of the engines! Then the gun stopped dead and the plane veered away from me and was lost to my view behind Windmill Hill, as it headed on towards Tidworth. I could hear the engines droning away into the distance. There must have been a lot of others having a go at them somewhere ahead, as I could hear a lot of sporadic shooting, but I was sure I had got the first shot at them, and that made me feel great!

I lowered the butt of the fifty calibre on its stop and, suddenly, felt exhausted. My throat and eyes burned from the smoky fumes from bullets. My wrists and arms, and the back of my neck, were very painful. I left the gun as it was and crept down below in my hideout and tried to wipe my eyes dry with spit on my handkerchief, and lay down and lit a fag. Sod that, I thought, that's hard work! It was all over in seconds, but I had, at last, had my wish and fired the fifty calibre at some Gerries!

I must have dropped off to sleep through exhaustion, because I didn't wake up till midday and, suddenly, I felt washed out and very hungry! I had better go out and cover the gun up. I'll clean it later and re-load if I can. I would have to lay low, anyway, for a while because all the activity that had been going on during the early morning would result in some patrols driving around the area. So, I thought I had better look at the fifty calibre and see why it had suddenly stopped firing. It turned out to be a misaligned cartridge in the belt and I had a job putting it right, so, as there were only a few rounds left, I decided to replace it with a new belt, which, again, was one hell-of-a-job on my own!

I cleaned out the barrel and loaded up, ready in case there was another action stations. I put on more camouflage round the gun emplacement and decided to go home at about four o'clock and call it a day, taking rations and an empty water can to get it re-filled for my next visit to the hideout!

Another week went quickly by, during which time there was plenty to do at work. They whole war machine seemed to be gathering momentum, and my mates at work and I were working on our different jobs, doing our best to help keep the mechanised and armoured vehicles ready for delivery to the troops.

JIM STOODLEY'S PRIVATE WAR

The next Sunday I decided to got out and shoot a few hares on my own, so I took the short Lee Enfield rifle and fifty rounds of ammo in a bandoleer. I had to make an early start to avoid being seen, so I departed from 1 South View at 4.30 a.m.

I headed out to the back of Perham Down, and was nearing the far end of a huge U.S. Army vehicle park, when a large hare came sauntering across my path, at about 200 yards distant. I unslung my Lee Enfield and put a shell up the spout. With this particular rifle, you could get nine rounds in the magazine and one loaded. The ground was dry and the time was, by now, about 6.00 a.m. I fired a marker shot at the hare and, immediately, it started off, full pelt! I could always hit a moving target better than a stationary one and, on the third shot, I stopped the hare in its tracks!

As I ran towards it to make the pick-up, two bullets sprayed the dust just ahead of me! This brought me to an abrupt halt! I looked over to my left and, some distance away, was an American sentry, waving his hands to me! I stood dead still and waved him over to where I was standing. He approached me, cautiously, carrying his rifle at the ready!

Now, my experience in dealing with the American soldiers was this; no way do you make any false moves and, in the circumstances I was in, it was best to let him have his say first!

"What the hell are you doing on U.S. Army property, and what's your name?" he growled, "You look like a Kraut!"

"Listen, mate," I said, "this here so-called U.S. Army property is part of my backyard! My name is Bud Flanagan, and I might have a big head, but I ain't no Gerry!"

"What the hell you doing here a-firing that goddam antique rifle, anyway?" he asked.

"Gis a fag mate!" I said.

"She-it! I you ain't got a nerve!" he gasped.

"Look, mate, I have been employed by the British Government to keep down these pests so they don't damage the crops! I'm allowed to keep any meat for myself and sell the skins, as they're valuable!"

He took out a pack of Camel, offered me one and took one himself, then stood there weighing me up, not sure he should believe me!

"Seems to me you have a good job, but why the hell you up at this hour, anyway?"

"Here you are, mate, have a light," I said. "Best time to shoot 'em, mate. They can't run as fast and, early in the morning, they're kind of dozey and can't spot you creeping up on them! Anyway, have you ever tasted English hares?"

"What's that? A kind of jack-rabbit?"

"Yes," I nodded, "here, let's walk on over and pick it up and you can take it back to the cook-house, get it skinned carefully, and sell the skins to any farmer in the area! Do you know, each good skin fetches ten bucks here in England, because of the fur? It's used to line the boots for the land-girls in winter."

"What's land-girls?" he queried, as he walked over to the dead hare. "How old are they, and what do they do?"

I explained to him what land-girls did, and this interested him very much. He was beginning to become friendly, now I had mentioned the great adaptability of some land-girls, and then I picked up the hare. It was a large one and I handed it to him.

"Here, it's yours, mate. I don't give these away to everyone, you know!"

"Gee, thanks, buddy! My name's Chuck. Glad to know you Bud!" he said, shaking my hand.

My Christ! I thought, what a bloody monicker!"

He took the hare from me and as he held it up, inspecting it, the blood was dripping on his boots, but he didn't notice that, he was just pleased to be the owner of the 'jack-rabbit', with a ten-dollar skin, and a good lunch to boot!

As he walked, slowly, back over the field he suddenly stopped and said, "Say, Bud, I really can't take this here jack-rabbit, it's worth too much dough!"

"Well, if it make you feel better, give me five bucks and you make five on the skin when you sell it, and have a real slap-up chow!"

"Well, yes, that's fine by me but, wait, I don't think I've got five bucks on me, I've got some English pounds!"

"Yeah, that's okay, just give me five, that's plenty!"

"You sure, Bud?" he said.

"Yeah, I'm sure, go ahead, be my guest!"

"Any chance of you letting me have some shells, Bud, as the Orderly Officer will check my shells as I come off guard at seven-thirty!"

"Yeah, here you are, take ten of mine."

"No, I don't need ten, only fired two at you. Well, you know what I mean, not at you . . ."

"Sure, I know what you mean," I interrupted, "but keep some spare so next time you're on guard duty and see some hares you can make yourself some more dough!"

"Thanks, Bud, that's some deal! So-long, I may see you around again! he said, as he walked away.

Not if I see you first, mate, I thought, and made a hasty retreat!

Since the sneak raid by the two Dorniers, more elaborate anti-aircraft gun defences were sited at different positions all over Salisbury Plain. Some were 40mm. Bofors guns, and others of a heavier calibre but I, myself, knew that the Dorniers that I saw had already dropped their bombs on Southampton thirty-odd miles away, and sneaked in low over the camps at Tidworth and Perham Down just to straff with their machine-guns, but one of them must have had a heck of a shock when he got a long burst from my 50 calibre!

It was my habit to visit the hideout on Windmill Hill at weekends and, as I hadn't spent a night there for a few days, I decided to go up on the Saturday evening. I was dying to tell my pals that I had fired at the Gerries, but I knew I couldn't, so I had to keep most of my movements secret. I decided to leave late at night with my fresh water supplies tied to my old bike and a few extras I might need over the weekend. John and I had a row earlier, so he did not go with me. He had a habit of sulking for days on end.

After dark, I set off with no lights on my bike. It would be best to go up Central Street, down Deweys Lane, past the recreation ground and allotments, and straight across the road to the Church, then a quick right and left and up to Collingbourne Bridge, then up through the Camp at Windmill Hill, and over the top and beyond, down to my hideout. In the distance, towards Southampton, I could see the searchlights scanning the sky. It was a chilly night, and I pushed on, eager to reach my hideout!

I knew my way, instinctively, in the dark and carefully hid my bicycle nearby. It was almost midnight and I decided to get right into bed. That meant lying full length on the floor with a few GI blankets under and over me. As I lay there, on that hard chalk floor, alone, at midnight, in the middle of Salisbury Plain, I wondered what it was that compelled me to push myself on to the limits all the time, dicing with death, but I couldn't help it, I wanted adventure! I needed it so badly! It was like a hungry man who had to eat. I had this insatiable hunger for dangerous living!

I lay awake that night, thinking how I could sneak across the Channel, armed to the teeth, and attack the enemy in the pill-boxes, giving them a taste of their own medicine. Sleep would bring me peace until the next daybreak.

I awoke, early, on the Sunday morning, about 6.00 a.m. I wanted to lie-in a bit longer, but I had to have a pee. What an effort! Getting up, folding the blankets and then getting out and stretching my legs!

What could I have for breakfast today? I had such a choice of food that I didn't know where to start! I lit up the old primus and first made a good mug of coffee. I had tins of Spam, real American Spam, in the food store, tins of tomato, orange and fruit juice, powdered egg, milk and pounds of brown sugar, tins of various meats, hams and curried beans (the kind that keep cowboys moving). It wasn't wise to eat too many of them, because, if you farted in the dug-out, with no ventilation, it would gas you out!

In the end, I settled for brown bread toast, with thick marmalade spread over, and liberal cups of black, sweet coffee to wash it down! I sat there content.

It was a little cold outside, unusual for this time of year, so I dressed up in my warm 'army gear'. I'd go for a walk, taking the sub-machine gun with me. I'd never leave the hideout without a weapon if I was walking over the Downs. If the Germans invaded, or paratroops dropped around me, I would always be ready for them!

I reached up to the shelf and unwrapped the 'greasegun', took down four spare magazines, thumbed in the ·45 shells until all four were full, and slid them in my ammo pouch. Deep down inside me something was nagging me, but what? I didn't know but today, nevertheless, I felt I should be more cautious! I glanced at my trusty Bulova (its owner was still in the Stockade), it was 7.30 a.m. and I made ready to go on my usual walk around.

I stepped out of the cover of the firs onto the open ground, my greasegun in my left hand. I'd better loose off half-a-dozen shots at the fir plantation opposite, just to test it. The bullets would not carry that far, as the pines were nearly a quarter-of-a-mile away. I fired away a few shots. At that moment I was about twenty feet away from my pines.

Suddenly, out of the blue, without warning, a fifty calibre opened up on me from the direction where I had fired! I could see the dust kick up all around me! Then the firing stopped!

I stood there, dumbfounded, rooted to the ground. From the fir trees opposite appeared two U.S. soldiers, each doing a short run, stop, run and zig-zag towards me, rifles at the ready!

A little voice in my brain said 'move it', and I did! I dived back into the sanctuary of my firs and hid myself from their view. As I did so, another stream of bullets from the fifty calibre came slicing through, just over my head, cutting off branches and splintering my face with pine-needles. I peered out, cautiously, through the undergrowth, and could see the two soldiers running back to their wood. Stupid bastards, them Yanks, I thought, they'll shoot at anything, never thinking of asking your name!

Apparently, while I was asleep that night, they had set up a machine-gun post in the opposite wood, possibly since the air-raid they were getting touchy, and, as I said before, strengthening their air defence.

I took another peep from my concealed position. The two soldiers had now stopped short and one knelt down and fired his rifle several times. He must have been practising, because he certainly couldn't see me. Silly sod! I lay still, thinking my hideout was finished now, the games up, and I'd lose all the grub and equipment, though there was a chance they may not find it, but the most pressing problem was how to get out of here in one piece! At that distance away from them, I could run back through my pines, back through the others, along the railway cutting and away home. There was still one chance left. Would they fail for the 'jack-rabbit' tale, like the sentry did? It's worth a try! I unbuckled my bandoleer of ammo, dropped my greasegun below in the grass, and walked calmly out, just a few feet into the open, waving my arms and shouting "What the hell you playing at? I'm English, you silly sods!"

For my efforts I received another hail of bullets from the fifty calibre, and several shots from the crouching soldiers!

Stupid sods! I thought, where were you when the bloody Dorniers came over? Bastard Yanks! They've no right here anyway! I belted back to my fifty calibre gun pit, pulled off the camouflage and covers, and stood up on the empty boxes. I'll give them rookies a few cookies right up their arses as a parting gift!

I looked out across to the other pines and, plain as day, there they were, advancing again! Oh, you want to play, eh? Well let's see how you duck this lot, mate! I pulled back the cocking handle and took a bead on the tree-tops to their right, squeezed the trigger, and fired a burst for five seconds. They immediately fell flat on their faces!

One GI got up and ran back to shelter. I gave him a short burst to keep him company, that really made him sprint! I fired another short burst and watched the tracer arc well over the fir trees. Then the other fifty calibre opened fire again in my direction. With lead flying perilously close to me, I fired again, and could see my tracers bouncing off the edge of their position, sending branches of the trees flying! I made sure my shooting was high, as I didn't want to hit anyone. These guys must have mistaken me for a parachutist or something, and when I first let off a few rounds to check the greasegun, they must have thought I was firing at them, and they, as usual, lost no time in shooting back!

I had fired a full belt of one hundred rounds over the past few minutes, and the gun stopped firing, leaving an uncanny silence. I knew now that

I had to get away fast! I knew I could outrun them, but I needed a good mile start to get beyond the range of their fifty calibre. I crawled out of the gun pit on my hands and knees, went to the hideout a few feet away, and collected my field glasses, as many fags as I could stuff in my jacket, my other bits and pieces, and crawled on to the far side of the firs, away from the 'enemy'. I would pick up my bike another time. I was sure they wouldn't find it, as I had hidden it well. The GIs were still firing a few odd rounds off, but they could not see me.

I ran across to the other pine wood, and then to the next and, by this time, I was well out of range, and sight. I ran on through the railway cutting and, eventually, arrived back home, undetected, though a bit dishevelled. There would be no more adventures out on Windmill Hill for me until things died down a bit!

I had a quick bath and change of clothing before Sunday dinner, which Mum was busy cooking over the paraffin cooker. Luckily, Dad was still at work!

"You'll have to stop sleeping out at nights, Jim, as Dad is shouting about it. So, in future, you have to be in the house by ten-thirty, sharp! Is that clear?"

"Oh, all right, Mum!" I answered.

CHAPTER 22

A Cabin In The Sky

OVER the railway lines, about half-a-mile from home, John and I had built a log cabin, high up in a giant oak tree. The trunk was unusual because for twenty-five feet from the ground, it went straight up and then large boughs branched out equally, then upwards, like giant flag-poles, and where they all branched out from the trunk, there was almost a flat platform, where it was possible for us to put down a floor and build a wall of logs, supported at four corners by the upright branches. This was an ideal fortification and, being so high off the ground, a very good observation post!

We finally completed the cabin after spending many hours of cutting down small saplings and hauling them up the tree on ropes. Then came the day to fit the flat roof and this, also, was basically silver birch three-inch diameter logging. We fixed up a heavy pulley to overhang from above the roof of the cabin on a strong beam, so that we could lift up any 'supplies' and 'ammo', because this was to be another hide-out and stronghold to fight the Germans if they decided to invade us, and being so high off the ground, and enclosed by the vertical boughs, it was well camouflaged and difficult to see!

In order to keep inquisitive people away, and from climbing the trunk, I put some grease around the tree-trunk, so it was impossible for anyone to climb up. We always took a rope and hook with us whenever we visited the cabin, so all we had to do to get up to our cabin was to throw up the hook until it anchored on a high branch and, then, climb up on the rope and retrieve it behind us.

I kept an old telescope in the cabin, which was very powerful, and on a clear day I could see very well indeed in all directions. I decided to keep at least a thousand rounds of ·45 bullets for the two sub-machine guns hidden in the cabin, and many C and K rations as a standby for emergencies! This was, if you like, an extension of our hideout on Windmill Hill, in case things got rough up there! Like they had, just recently, when the Yanks chased me out!

The one advantage of our cabin was that it was not as far from home as the outpost on Windmill Hill, and there were plenty of pheasants and wood-pigeons at certain times of the year, which always made a tasty meal!

Across a couple of fields, about five-hundred yards from the cabin, was a poultry and pig farm. This belonged to Mr Watton, and one of his sons was Len who used to go to the same school as me. Len worked full-time now, on the farm and he worked very hard. Even late on the summer evenings, Len could be seen toiling away on some job or other, out on the farm. Some nights he would come over to the cabin and we would have a 'fry-up' on our primus up in the treetops, and have a Lucky Strike cigarette. We would take it in turns to tell our version of the latest dirty jokes. Some evenings we would sit up there, late into the night and, after having a big fry-up with the eggs which Len brought over from his Dad's farm, and any bread and marg supplemented from the K-rations, we would sit and talk about our school days.

Len was on the tall side. Wiry and very good-natured, and liked a joke, but would not get involved with any of my illicit activities. He didn't mind smoking the fags and eating the rations I pinched and, on a rare occasion, would come for a cross country ride with me in a 'borrowed' U.S. Army scout car, or a Greyhound armoured vehicle.

Many a night, you could hear the uncanny throb of the enemy aircraft high up in the black sky, passing over on their way to some raid up country, and, on the odd occasion, you could hear a night fighter firing at one of these invisible raiders.

As this cabin was close to the village, it was too dangerous to use any firearms so, for a change, our home-made bows and arrows were a nice diversion. Many a happy hour was passed, shooting from the roof of the cabin, lying flat on our backs, firing at the slow-whirling seagulls, or the odd crow which flew across our field of five. But the diversions were few and far between.

Our country was in the middle of a deadly struggle for survival. I knew how I would react to enemy troops dropping down around me! There was no tomorrow for me, just today. I had vowed, long before, that I would fight to my last bullet and I hoped that I would last long enough to kill plenty of them first, also, since my plans to kill Hitler had gone adrift, I had to make sure the best of whatever opportunity that came along.

There were plenty of gullies and hedgerows around Ludgershall and, if their tanks came my way, I had a bazooka ready for them! This weapon was deadly at close range, and simplicity itself to operate. I had watched the U.S. 29th Infantry Division, whilst training with them, and I had one hidden in the air-raid shelter at home. I told Mum it was an exhaust pipe off a tank, when she tripped over it one day!

"Well, get it out of here, will you, Jim? Someone's going to break their neck, especially if they come down in the dark. I don't know, the places you hide things!" she remonstrated.

"All right, Mum," I replied sheepishly. So I ended up hiding it under my bed, which was not a bad place, because when, and if, the time came to use it, I had an ideal position to fire it from. The bedroom window!

Some evenings, when I was a bit bored, I would open my bedroom window and rest the bazooka on the window ledge and take aim on any cars or trucks that passed the house on the main road below, and on the corner of the road junction was a letter-box, which made a good aiming point for practising. Also from by bedroom window, I could see our cabin in the distance, and sometimes, could just make out our flag, high up on its pole.

John and I had several codes, one being that if the flag was at half-mast, it meant that one of us was in trouble, or the Gerries were landing (enemy in sight) or something like that, in which case, we would race over to the cabin and take up our defensive positions.

After a few weeks, word got around that we had some guns up in the cabin, and various warlike stores. The local bobby came over there in our absence and got a lot of grease on his uniform, trying to climb up the tree-trunk, that made him mad, as he did not manage to get up and he then went to see Dad, making the usual complaints and dragging in the farmer who owned the field, who, in the past, had turned a blind eye to our antics on his property.

In the end, Dad went over and took a look for himself, from ground level and, with the help of the local constabulary, decided it should come down and that we should, in future, keep away from the place, but first we had to destroy it.

This upset me and John, as we had put one heck of a lot of work into building it. Still, nevertheless, orders are orders, so we promised to take it apart in the very near future. With that, things looked quieting down somewhat.

We were all sitting down to tea at home, Dad at his usual place at the end of the table. He had been giving John and I a good telling-off because we had not yet dismantled the cabin, which I had promised to do about three weeks before but, somehow had not got around to it yet, and I thought he might have forgotten about it by now. Dad started to make himself quite clear.

"Now, look, you two. Both of you will get a bloody good-hiding if that's not pulled down in the next few days. Is that clear?"

"Yes, Dad," we both piped up together.

"Well, make sure you do, or there will be some big trouble!"

John and I finished our tea and sauntered out into the garden and, sitting on the fence, started to plan the best way to go about it when brother Bob jumped off the bus at the stop outside the house. He walked up the path towards us.

"Hello, you two. How you doing? Have you had your tea yet?"

"Course we have," I replied, "ain't none left for you!" He laughed and slapped me over the head as he walked past.

"I'm on leave for a couple of days, so you'd better behave or else I'll put a few armlocks on you!"

"Oh, yeah! You and who else is going to help you, then?" I sneered as he disappeared into the house.

A plan started to hatch in my head. Now, if Bob had recently transferred to the Airborne Regiment from the Black Watch and was doing all this special training and things, he may be the answer to our prayer!

Bob was about nineteen, tough and extra cocky. He was always bragging about the things he used to do when he went on these special missions, but, for all that, if you gave him a bit of soft-soap, he would always do you a favour. There was a strong possibility that, if the worst came to the worst, we could bribe him with a few quid, as his pay in the army was only buttons. So, later on that night, I took him out up the backyard and approached the subject of the cabin. We both sat down on the top of the air-raid shelter.

"Look, Bob," I said, "you know the log cabin we have up in the tree over the railway, don't you? Well, we have to get rid of it! Dad's kicking up all sorts of hell about it and we have to pull it down soon as we can. We've put a lot of work into it but it's got to go!" Bob sat there looking at me with that usual mischievous look in his eyes.

"Well," he replied, "what do you want me to do about it? Blow it up or something! Anyway, what's in it for me?"

"Well, as a matter of fact, I was going to ask you that, but I think it's too big a job, as it would need a lot of planning, and too much explosive, I think!"

"Don't you believe it!" he retorted, "I've blown up bloody great buildings and all kinds of bridges in the army. That job would be simple enough!"

"Would it, Bob?"

"Yes! I'll send it sky-high for you. Tree and all if you want!"

"That's good of you, Bob. How much would you need to do the job?"

"What?" Explosives?" he asked.

122

"No. Money I mean!"

"Oh!" his face turned serious, "I think I could manage that for, say, three quid. But I want paying first, before the job!"

"Of course!" I replied, "I'll get half off John and give it to you tonight. Is that okay?"

"Yeah, that's all right. As a matter of fact, I've got a date tonight with Alma Brown, and I could do with a few shillings. You get the dough, Jim, and we'll go up there this Sunday afternoon. Meanwhile, I'll get the explosives and bits I need tomorrow and we'll set off the charge after dark on Sunday night, but don't say a word to anyone. Tell John the same, Okay?"

"Fair enough, Bob. Don't worry, we'll keep quiet!" and I went and got the other thirty-shillings from John, after explaining what the plan was. John seemed satisfied and handed over his bit, saying: "I hope it works properly, Jim!"

"Of course if will, John," I went on, "there's a bloody guarantee, anyway, on the job. You know Bob. He's too cocky for it to fail, isn't he? So, let him think he's the expert and don't upset him while he's home on leave or he might 'welsh' on the deal, especially if he's got our dough!"

That Sunday afternoon arrived and, true to his word, Bob arrived home just after lunch with an ominous knapsack slung over his shoulder! We made our way, furtively, by a round-about route to the cabin. I brought along my rope and hook so that we could climb up the tree, and soon both of us were sitting in the cabin, with me putting all my hidden stores into sacks and lowering them down the tree and, temporarily hiding them in a haystack at the other end of the field, until I could find a safer place!

"Where in hell did you get all that gear from?" Bob gasped, as he set about fixing the explosives in various corners of the cabin.

"Oh, I got a bit here and there, you know," I replied.

"No wonder the bloody cops are after you!" he muttered, as he put the finishing touches on the slow fuses.

This setting off the explosives was fairly dangerous, as the detonators, which Bob pushed into each wad of plasticine-like explosive, before inserting the fuse-wire, were liable to go off without any prompting. As Bob said, some were faulty, and I was glad when we both finally swung down the escape rope to the ground! But, as the cabin was about twenty-off feet off the ground, there was not enough fuse to reach down, and it was then that Bob told me each three fuse wires were of only about twenty-five seconds! So, later on in the evening, when we went back to explode the charges, there was not going to be much time to light the fuses and retire to a fairly safe distance!

It was dark, about 7.00 p.m. and with a full moon, which gave a little light for us when we returned to the cabin. So, this was to be the big bang!

I was trembling with excitement as I hauled myself up the rope behind Bob and when we, finally, reached the cabin, we sat down and I had a smoke, while Bob told me the plan. We would light one fuse by holding the match-box along the match, so that the flame of it lighting would be strong enough to light the fuse. Bob would have the tricky job of lighting the two other fuses in the same way but, as soon as I lit mine, I was to grab the escape rope, slide down fast, and run like hell down the hedgerow! Bob would be right behind me, counting off the seconds, and would shout when he thought we should hit the ground and take cover!

Bob stood up and re-checked the fuses and put on one of his serious looks.

"Now, look, Jim. Listen carefully! When I say light your fuse, do it right away! If it doesn't light first time, don't try to light another. Is that clear? Because you won't have time, and don't wait around buggering about with it. Now, take your match out and wait for the word!" Bob nodded to me and took out his matches and we both got ready to strike up!

Over at Mr Watton's farm Len had not long finished his tea and was doing the usual nightly rounds, like closing the chicken run and making sure all the pigs were bedded down for the night. He didn't mind these extra chores in the evening and it was, after all, a nice evening, with a nice bright moon to give him light to finish his job comfortably.

He looked over in the direction where the cabin stood. He could just make out its outline. I wonder where Jim is tonight, he thought, as he sat down on a meal bin and lit a fag. He could see the flag hanging, limply, on its mast. Everything was quiet. Too quiet, Len thought, and he walked the few feet to the gate and sat astride the cross-bar.

"Ready, Jim?" Bob called out.

"Ready as I'll ever be!" I replied.

"Okay, Jim. Strike now!"

I lit my fuse and it fizzed into life first go. I was out on to the escape rope and down to the ground so fast that the rope burned my hands, and I raced away down the hedgerow, like the clappers. I glanced over my shoulder and Bob was just getting on the rope to come down to earth a few seconds behind me!

I ran on, as if my life depended on it. I could hear Bob pounding behind, calling out between gasping breath: "Run . . . Run . . . Go like hell!" and go like hell I did!

124

Across two fields, and still perched on the gate, Len took a long drag at his fag, his gaze once more rested on the cabin. Only the odd grunts and cackle from the sheds nearby stirred the silence. Suddenly, a blinding flash seared the night sky! Followed by a terrific explosion, which, like a large invisible hand, seemed to swipe him over backwards off the gate! He landed in a heap in a load of pig shit!

Meanwhile, back at the cabin, Bob and I had already hit the deck and were covering our heads and hoping the falling debris would miss us!

"Come on, Jim!" Bob called, after most of the dust had settled, "let's get away as far as we can, before they start looking around over here!" With that, we made a run for home, the longest way round. Looking back, occasionally, I could see a large void where once stood the cabin and a few flames were visible behind the dense smoke!

Back at the farm, Len started to crawl to the galvanised tin fence to try to get some sort of protection from the bits and pieces that were falling down all around him. Jesus Christ! he thought, what a bloody mess I'm in! Bits were still landing around him and he could hear a few panes of glass breaking on the greenhouse roof!

Mr Watton came rushing out the back door and ran down the path to find Len picking himself off the ground.

"What was that, Len?"

"I'll give you one guess, Dad!" Len replied. "That was Jim Stoodley's tree-house blown sky-high. Look at the state of me!" Len was trying to wipe the dirt off his clothes.

"Yes, I'll bet my last shilling our Jim has got a little bored and decided to liven things up!"

"I hope the young sod was up there when it went up!" Len's Dad replied. "Wait till I see his Dad. He won't be very pleased with him when I give him the bloody bill for this lot of damage! That's if it was his doing, and there's no doubt he'll deny being anywhere near here. Will he?"

"Well, I suppose you can't blame him, Dad, unless it was him, but if you like, I'll ask him tomorrow, when I see him.

Mr Watton went back into the house, mumbling all kinds of horrible things he was going to do to Jim Stoodley, if he was the culprit, and called to Len to get a bath and a change of clothes. Len walked to the end of the chicken run and, as he stared across, he could still see the smoke and one or two little flames flickering.

Mr Watton asked my Dad if I had anything to do with the big bang the night before, and so did the local bobby, but I made sure I had a cast-iron alibi. I was not going to be roped in on this one! Dad knew it was me, after all, had he not asked me several times to get the cabin moved out of it, so I suppose he thought that it was a blessing in disguise that it had eventually gone. So, after a while, things calmed down.

CHAPTER 23

Sergeant Closky And His Depot "Scotch"

I MET Sgt Closky of the Service of Supply (S.O.S.) corps at the Depot. He was about twenty-three years old, short and stocky, and hailed from Alabama. He was a typical 'way-down-south' type. I got on very well with him, even if he did call me a 'limey' sometimes, and I called him a 'reb'. It was while I was on temporary duty at Brimstone Bottom that I met him.

Now, Sgt Closky had a weakness and that was he liked spirits a great deal! In fact, he couldn't get enough of it! Not that he wanted to drink it all himself. He liked to share it with others, but at a price! So, he devised a plan where he would acquire a steady supply of surgical spirit from the U.S. military infirmary and as he was, at that particular time, in charge of the fire-extinguisher (tetrachloride) store, which was a concrete bunker-type building, remote from the rest of the workshops and 'admin' buildings, it was ideal for blending is ill-gotten gains in among the drums of tetrachloride.

He had a small office at one end, and used to sit at his desk, mostly all the day, totting up his orders and his profits, always smoking his cigar. He always kept a few bottles of 'Depot Scotch' under his desk, for the casual customer who came in.

I used to slip in to his office for a chat nearly every day, and he would tell me all about his home town back in the States. He loved to recall his earlier days on the Tombigbee River and used to believe he was another Tom Sawyer of Mark Twain fame, as he talked away, flicking his cigar ash down the end of his desk, there must have been a leaky bottle of 'Scotch' because, suddenly Sgt Closky and his desk were engulfed in flames! I had been sitting on a 'tet' drum, surrounded by hundreds of gallons of fire-extinguisher fluid and pyrene fire-extinguishers. He jumped off his chair shouting "Goddam it! Put me out!" As he spun round in a panic, I grabbed an extinguisher and sprayed his legs and table and, very quickly, put the fire out. Sgt Closky got away with only singed eyebrows and moustache, and a scorched ego!

"Gee, thanks, Jim. Sure glad you were here with me. You save my Depot Scotch going up in smoke!" He wasn't worried about his own safety one bit! He managed to keep the incident from reaching the higher echelons and I helped him clear the store up.

Brimstone Bottom, 1994. Sergeant Closky's "Depot Scotch Distillery" still stands (centre picture). (Photo: Courtesy Frank Gamble, 1994)

He used to charge five dollars a bottle for his 'invention' which was mixed with either Coke or Pepsi! It was a deadly potent drink! I was not a drinker and never sampled it, but many GIs and their girlfriends did, to their cost, as, taken in larger doses than a teaspoonful, it would blow the top of your head off!

I went to a dance at the social club at the Depot and it was here that Sgt Closky made a lot of dough selling his depot 'Scotch' to all his buddies, and anyone else who fancied a stiff drink out of the ordinary! Many of the English girls there took a few of them and, after drinking one or two of Closky's wares, they would shoot their legs and arms out stiff as a board and pass out until next morning, when they would wake up with one mother-and-father of a headache. In one or two extreme cases there were some fatalities. After seeing some of the bad effects caused by the drink which was supplied by Sgt Closky, I decided that I would try and exert some pressure on him, by trying to get him to, at least, 'water' his 'Scotch' down, so its effects would not be too bad. Among other things, this carry-on was very bad for the war effort. When I threatened to shop his activities to the MPs, however, he promised to do as I asked and used less surgical spirit in his depot 'Scotch'!

I had many a happy dinner break with him, though, because on a few occasions he would take a Harley Davidson and give me a ride over the Downs, or perhaps, on the odd times, got into Andover, seven miles away, and sitting on the large 'buddy-seat' behind him on a warm sunny day was really a treat not to be missed! But as time went on I noticed a sharp change take place in Closky. He would be late for work sometimes, and he missed a shave, which was very odd, as the Closky I once knew was always well turned out. I put this down to the extra booze he was knocking back, even at work. I didn't quite know how to tackle him about this apparent problem he must have had, but one evening I went up to the barracks and he was sitting on his bed reading.

"Hello, Vernon," I greeted him, as I walked up to where he sat.

"Hi, Jim," he answered, sitting up and putting his book on the bed beside him, "What d'ya know?"

"Not much, but I'll tell you what, Vernon, I am glad I caught you here tonight, because I want to talk to you on a delicate matter!" Closky tipped his peaked cap back a little on his head and looked inquiringly at me.

"Yes, sure, Jim. Go ahead. Shoot! What can I do to help?"

"Well, you see, Vernon, I wondered if you had some sort of trouble back home or, you know, some kind of problem . . ."

"Look, Jim, get to the point. What are you trying to say? I got problem? I ain't got no problem, no siree! You got the goddam problems, according to the stories I hear about you from the guys in the Motor Pool!" Closky was getting annoyed.

"Look, Vernon," I pressed on, "I am, as you can plainly see, just a young lad, but I've seen a change in you this last few weeks, and I am, as a considered friend of yours I hope, worried about you. Now, if you wanna get all chewed up about that, well, should I bother?"

Closky leaned over to his locker and took a cigar from a large box in the top drawer. He sat back against the wall as if to support what he was about to say to me.

"Look, Jim, don't get me wrong. I appreciate having you as a friend, and you doing all this worrying about me. Sorry I appear to be a bit edgy, but I don't have many more worries than other guys here. We all got a job to do, I guess, and some of us do a little more bitching or worrying than others, and, anyway, I don't have no one back home, except my Pa, and I have not seen him for going on ten years. He took off when my Ma took a shotgun to him after she caught him shacking up with some gal from the drug store. Shortly after that she took an overdose of sleeping pills I think it was, so as you can see, Jim, you need not worry about me. Thanks, anyway, for being a good buddy and all that, but I sure don't need any guidance and them stripes on my arm there means I ain't no mug!

"No-one says you are, Vernon," I replied, "it's just that when I first met you a few months back you were a lot different, I mean you didn't drink anything like you do now, and you were always laughing and joking. Now, you seem to keep to yourself! You're late for work sometimes and don't always shave. I know it's nothing to do with me, Vernon, but you see I hear the guys talking a lot, and they seem to think you're about to go over the hill (absent without leave) so I'm only, sort of, letting you know what the other guys are saying behind your back, see!"

Closky shifted his position on the bed and stubbed out the butt of his cigar, then, looking at the remains, said: "You're bound to hear a lot of talk from the GIs here. A lot of them don't like me for a start. Jealous, that's what they are, Jim. Don't like to see me selling all this booze, and, let's be honest, most of them are goddam buck privates ain't they?"

"Well, I don't know about that, Vernon," I replied, "but, generally speaking, they all seem to think you are in some sort of trouble!"

"Trouble! I thrive on it, Jim. I'm used to that. It makes life a little bit more interesting, Jim, and it sure does pay off sometimes, specially if it concerns the good sales of Depot Scotch. You know how much I made last month on the 'Scotch' alone, Jim? Two thousand bucks, close on. Now, that's a lot of dough, ain't it?"

"I agree, Vernon, it is, but you would spend a hell of a long time in the guardhouse if one of them buck privates went to the Colonel and sang a song! What would all that dough do for you? If I were you, I would call it a day, Vernon, while you are ahead. I mean, you got your stripes to think about, to say the least, and it would mean a long lock-up job for you if you were caught, wouldn't it?"

"Aw, shit, Jim, you're always looking on the dull side of life. Anyway, listen who's talking! You're a fine example of a righteous bastard! You've stolen more vehicles and guns off the U.S. Army than they turn out in a month! You should be telling me not to do this or do that! By Christ, you take the goddam biscuit, and you ain't even in the army. I wouldn't mind so much if you were!" Closky took a bottle from under the bed and took a swig, wiped his mouth with the back of his hand, and said: "Have a drop of this, Jim, and stop worrying about me!"

"You know I never drink that stuff!" I replied.

"You don't know what's good for you. That will put some lead in your pencil!"

"I've got plenty already, Vernon! I replied.

"Now, listen, Jim. Take some advice from an old hand. Just let me take care of my own problems, as you call them. Look after yours. Okay?"

"Yes, all right, mate. I was only trying to be of some help!"

We talked about different things for a while, until I felt it was time for me to go home.

I continued to see Sgt Closky on several occasions. Meanwhile, Dad made one or two remarks to me about Closky's peculiar behaviour and slovenliness, and on one or two days he was the worse for drink. Dad would keep him out of sight until he sobered up, as the Captain in the Motor Pool was very strict, but, luckily was away on meetings more often than not. Dad was like that! He always liked to look after 'his men'.

Across from the office was a large parade ground in front of the hospital and, on this dinner break today, there was a U.S. Army band, practising, marching up and down, back and forth, really belting out some good tunes. I loved to watch and listen to them as often as I could and, today being nice and warm, was ideal, so I just sat back on the hood of a jeep and enjoyed the show. After about fifteen minutes the band stopped for a rest, and I walked over to where they were sitting down on the parade ground. I walked up to the Major and started to chat with him.

"I really enjoyed that, Sir," I said. He looked over to me and said: "I'm real pleased you did. You work around here, son?"

"Yes, sir," I replied, seeing my chance of striking up a friendship that could be very beneficial to me, if I played my cards right. "My Dad is in charge of the Motor Pool over there," I pointed as I spoke.

"Oh, that's nice," the Major replied, "You enjoy working with the U.S. Army?"

"It's great," I went on, "I get to drive a lot of trucks and it's a pleasure to be in the company of such a swell bunch of guys!"

The Major seemed very pleased by that remark and asked me if I had ever played any instruments.

"I've always been interested in the kettle-drum," I told him, "and I've always wanted to march in a band and twirl the sticks."

The Major, and some of the men, laughed and he then asked a tall bandsman with the drum to come across to where we sat.

"Here, son, would you like to strap this on? PFC Sands will show you how to put the brace on," and he indicated to the PFC to get me kitted up and he adjusted the straps as best he could.

"Now look, son," the Major went on, "we'll have another short practise and you can do your best to keep the beat up.

The Major called the men to parade and told me to go to the gap in the front, vacated by the drummer whose place I had taken. Most of the members of the band were smiling at me and giving me some encouragement and I felt really cocky out there in the front and ready to go!

I asked the Major if they would play *I'm a Yankee Doodle Dandy*.

"Sure," he replied. I watched the guy next to me lift his sticks and, with the roll of the drums, on the command, off we went across the parade ground. I soon found out that it was not as easy as it looked from the outside looking in, but I did my best to keep in step and in time with the drummer next to me.

I tried very hard to beat out some sort of rhythm and seemed to be doing fairly well, managing to hold on to the sticks without dropping them, my scalp tingling with excitement as we continued to the other end of the parade ground. Then we came to a halt. I had a suspicion that I was disrupting the rest of the band but as the Major walked up to me he made out that I had done well!

"Well, you seemed to handle that okay, son!" he said, as he helped to take the drum and harness off me, "anyway, you can tell your buddies that you have marched, and played, with a U.S. Army band, can't you?"

"Yes," I replied, "and thank you very much. I really enjoyed it!" With that, I walked back over to the Motor Pool office. Just then, Dad came out with his cup of tea in his hand.

"Did you like that, Jim?" he inquired, meaning my recent march with the band.

"Yes, I did."

"Well, you can get back to work now. Do you know you're late!"

"No, I didn't notice the time, Dad." I replied. "I'm sorry!"

"Okay. Get on with it then, son, and get those trucks checked to make sure they all have fire extinguishers!"

I walked over to the store room and pushed the door open. Closky was sleeping in the corner and the place reeked of cigar smoke and Depot Scotch! Oh, my God, I thought, not again! I knew it was no good trying to wake him. It was obvious he was well and truly sozzled, so I left him to it and went out to the truck-park to check them all, as Dad had requested.

This particular day dawned, very wet! I heard Dad's alarm clock ringing and jumped out of bed and looked out of the window. Outside the overnight rain had left large puddles on either side of the road and, as the traffic went by, it sprayed big sheets of water over the high banks which bordered the other side of the main Andover road. Those who were waiting for the bus had to run back to avoid getting soaked, each time a car or lorry went past! I'm lucky, I thought, I haven't got to wait out there, I shall get a lift into Perham with Dad.

Dad always prepared the toast and tea for our breakfast, while I used to go out and open the garage doors and start up the Talbot. This car was a little temperamental and it required two turns of the starting handle, with the choke out, and then she would always start, first time, when you pressed the starter! I would then drive the car out of the garage and, if the weather was extra cold, leave the engine running for five minutes, or so, and then go back in and eat my toast and drink my cup of tea. We had to be at work by eight o'clock and Dad always made sure that we left in good time, so that we were clocked-in promptly, with a few minutes in hand, but this particular morning was to herald some very sad news.

I went to the fire extinguisher store and unlocked the door. Sgt Closky was not yet in. He was usually late so I took the broom and generally tidied up the place. I then sat in Closky's chair and, looking out of the window, I could see all the activity, which was usually a repeat of the morning before! For example, most GIs would be seen taking hot mugs of coffee and doughnuts to their different offices or workshops, after a short wait in the queue at the mobile PX which was open at various times during the day.

I looked over to the far side of the vehicle park. Some drivers were connecting up their huge trailers to the tractors. They could be going to a number of places. Perhaps it may be to the docks at Southampton with a load of ammo, or it could be any kind of military stores to any part of the country. This was a busy place, as was any U.S. Army depot in time of war.

Yes, I suppose I had a bird's-eye view of everything from Closky's seat. I could make out Dad walking briskly across the road and I knew right away that he was heading to my store. I could see he had a very worried look on his face. He always wore the same peaked cap, always pulled well down. I knew he had seen me at the window. Perhaps I was going to get a telling-off for loafing around so early in the morning when there was so much to do! Well, I thought, it's no good me jumping up and making out I'm doing something now, he's seen me, so I will stay put in Closky's chair! I heard Dad open the outer door, then he was in the office. I could see, at once, that something was very wrong! I had seen that look before! He was slightly short of breath, as he sat down near me.

"Just had another bombshell!" this was one of Dad's favourite sayings!

"What's that, Dad?" I inquired.

Dad leaned back in the chair and took a deep breath, hands folded on his lap. I stared at them. He must have had the largest hands in the world, I thought, with very thick fingers to match. My gaze wandered back to his face again. His eyes were ice-cool blue and always seemed tired! After a short pause he spoke:

"Well, Jim, I have just had a phone call from HQ and they tell me that late last night Sgt Closky was killed in an accident on the railway line. It seems he must have been drunk, but I don't know the full details yet. I suppose I shall find out more soon!"

I was shocked, but not altogether taken by surprise! I always feared something like this might happen to him sooner or later!

Dad sat there in silence. He started to rub his hands, which he had a habit of doing when under stress. I always thought that if there were ten men like Dad, the war would be over in no time at all!

"I want you to get all Sgt Closky's things, Jim, everything that belongs to him in here and bring them to my office, right away."

Dad left and I watched him as he walked away back to the Motor Pool. It was the first time I had noticed his stoop, and tired walk. It was funny, I thought, you never seem to think about your Dad getting old. Never, ever, think that one day he will die and you would have to live the rest of your life without his guidance and strength to support you! I wondered why I was thinking these things, but they just went through my mind at the time!

I lifted up the top lid of Closky's desk and found a collection of papers and a large notebook. I opened it and inside was a list of his dealings and names of his customers, who he had sold, or intended to sell, his booze to! I tore this up into small pieces. It would not help if the investigating officers got hold of that! There was a box of his favourite cigars, a couple of packs of cigarettes and his lighter. There were also letters, some with lipstick on! As I searched through the various items, I began to feel the shock of his death come over me. I was not greatly attached to Closky, but I had known him fairly well and we had spent many hours talking and, as I said before, had been out with him on the Harley Davidson motorcycle.

I looked under his desk and there were his shoes, which he would change into when he arrived at work. A spare pair of his fatigues hung on the wall. I collected everything and put it neatly into a cardboard carton. At the back of my mind I was still wondering how he came to be on that railway line, but perhaps I would find out more from Dad when I called at the office with Closky's belongings. I looked around the office, thinking that no more would I see him here again and what could the guy who would replace him be like!

I eventually arrived at Dad's office and put the carton on his desk.

"Here you are, Dad," I said, sitting down opposite him. Dad took the cartoon and placed it in the corner.

"That's all, Jim?"

"Yes," I replied, trying to avoid the gaze of several of his buddies. There was an uncomfortable silence hanging over the place, as one would expect in the circumstances, I suppose, so I thought the best thing for me to do was go back to my store and get on with a few jobs.

There was no doubt about it, I would miss Closky and his little chats about the things he used to do back in the States. There was never a dull moment with him around. Even if he used to tell me lies sometimes, I didn't mind, because it was all so very interesting, and I learned a lot about the habits and different ways people live in the States. Closky seemed to me to be a fountain of knowledge, always using his hands to get his point over, and forever complaining about the easy life the officers had here in the UK!

I had just finished my dinner and was taking it easy after the hectic morning I had been through, after having to deal with the news of Sgt Closky, when Dad called around again with the whole story to date.

Closky had been seen out drinking by several people the night before and, it appeared he was fairly drunk when last seen outside a pub in Ludgershall. He had his Harley with him, and several of his buddies were trying to get him to leave his bike until he sobered up the following day. All this, however, was to no avail, as Closky was intent on riding it, shouting "Where's this goddam war? I'm going to start the Second Front! Any of you chicken-shits want to come along? Then hop on my buddy-seat!" Needless to say, no-one would take up the challenge, and eventually, Closky started his bike and, after a few wobbly false starts, careered off up the Everleigh road! It was not quite clear just how he got on to the Ludgershall to Tidworth railway line but, he did, and around midnight he rode his bike full pelt, head on, into the front of a goods train, which was loaded with army supplies, including tanks!

Not only did poor Closky lose his life, but his head as well, and that was not found until four hours later, fifty yards from the scene of the accident. His bike was just a tangled mass of scrap metal!

I just sat there, listening to Dad relate these sordid details to me, which I must admit dented even my strong constitution! Dad went on:

"I'm giving you the full gruesome details, Jim. You might as well hear them for me first-hand. It may help to bring home to you the dangers of what can happen when you have had too much to drink. You're better off without the bloody stuff and, in some way, I hope you will take note of what can happen!"

Dad got up and started to walk to the door, pulling at the peak of his cap as he went. He paused at the door, turned and said: "All these chances you continually take, Jim, messing around with these trucks and tanks, guns and all of these tricks you get up to! Just let this accident be an example to you of what can happen!"

I let Dad go on his way with no comment. I knew it would be useless, and a waste of time, to argue with him, and soon we moved back to the Motor Pool at Tidworth.

CHAPTER 24

Orderly Officer – Disorderly Latrine!

T HINGS were hotting up a bit at Tidworth Depot. More military stores were arriving daily and very large cases were being stacked into every bit of available space.

My Dad was organising convoys all over the country, with supplies of war materials, to various U.S. Army bases and, once a week, there were about forty trucks sent to Newbury, where there was a gigantic food storage depot, which kept all U.S. forces in the southern counties fed to the high standards required. Yes, America looked after her troops even in time of war, when things are expected to be in short supply. I can never remember a case where there was ever a shortage of food and, of course, the proverbial ice cream!

I must admit, I liked the Americans very much. Perhaps a lot of my admiration sprang from the fact that they were generous and, as it was hard times for us all in England. Through my boyish eyes I could see more advantages in being friendly with them than not. Still, I liked the way they operated, always on the ball, which was their favourite expression!

I had been given so many clothes at work by many of the soldiers, that I had a fairly good wardrobe of socks, real patent leather shoes, and silk scarves. The American soldiers liked silk very much! I had also spent so much time among them, that I began to think like them and believe I inherited many of their ways! But back to the Depot: I was busy myself too! Dad was not a hard taskmaster, but he saw to it that everyone under his supervision did their whack and that included me as much as anyone!

The great thing about my job was that here I was in the middle of one of the largest arsenals of mixed army stores in England. Every type of vehicle, tracked and wheeled and amphibious, motorcycles, artillery pieces, almost every type of equipment the United States supplied to its army was here, and I could ride it, drive it, float it and, at the worst, wreck it!

For the use of the 'brass' at the Depot there was a fleet of several Chrysler, Buick, Ford, Chevrolet and Pontiac cars. All but the Chryslers were dressed in olive drab paint. One of the black Chrysler Imperials was the Colonel's car and I had to make sure that it was always gassed up and clean. This was a straight eight-cylinder job and what a car!

The Colonel had just returned, the night before, from a two-day trip and the Chrysler was covered in mud, so this morning meant a trip to the washrack on the large car park at the south end of the Depot, behind the tank shop. The washrack was in the middle of the park and the compressor for the pressure water hose was right next door, and part of, the gents latrines, which were normally (after 'the night before') engaged!

Now, in this Depot, there was a certain Major Allen who was, today, acting as Officer of the Day. I knew him, and he knew me! I'd had a skirmish with him one day when he had, quite wrongly, crossed a stop line in the Depot and dented the back of a jeep I was driving. He had called me a stupid Limey and I had called him a stupid fat son-of-a-bitch! He didn't like it, so he tried his best to make things awkward to me. Major Allen did not know it, but today he would meet his Water-LOO!

I could see Dad walking over to the garage where I was working, his flat peaked cap on his head. His step seemed urgent as he walked up to me, a little out of breath.

"Why aren't you down the washrack cleaning that bloody car, Jim?"

"I'm just off now, Dad!" I replied.

"You're always 'just going' to do something! Now, hurry up! Wash the Chrysler and no joy-riding round the bloody countryside in it! And get back soon, and chamois and polish it!"

I got into the car and drove away. What a car, I thought, one day I'll own one after the war. Oh, I was always going to do something 'after the war'!

I cruised slowly down past the Colonel's office. I knew that, if he happened to be looking out, he would see me driving his car by, carefully, and that would please him. I left the Colonel's stars on the car and a few troops saluted the car as it passed along the main "drag" to the washrack, thinking that the Colonel would be inside! It made me feel very important and I'd salute back sometimes, then they would realise it was me pulling their legs and feel rather foolish and gave me a 'V'-sign. In return they received two from the driver!

I had now passed the large tank repair workshops and drove on towards the washrack, not far now, the engine on this big car purring effortlessly. So quiet, a dream to drive. Again, I thought I would own one like this one day after the war. It was always 'after the war' that one felt things would be better, but the end never seemed to be in sight.

I had now arrived at the washrack, and could see a jeep parked near the pump-house, flying the flag of the Officer of the Day. No! Not that sly sod! I wonder where he is! Not a sign of him anywhere.

138

I pulled up in front of the pump-house alongside a nine-ton light tank, sometimes called the M5, or 'Stuart'. This tank, for the technically minded, was nine tons and usually sported a two-pounder gun, or snub-nosed 37mm Howitzer and, later on, various modifications, guns of different calibres. Two V8 Cadillac 8.2-litre engines, in tandem, propelled this little marvel along at a top speed of, sometimes, 40 mph through a General Motor hydramatic auto transmission, with five forward speeds and one reverse. Rubber cleats were fitted onto the tracks.

As I got out of the Chrysler, I noticed that the engines on the tank were still running, but I could see no sign of the driver. I had never been inside this model and I thought that, as there was no-one in sight, I would like to climb in and have a look! But, first, I had better get the pressure hose out and wash the Colonel's Chrysler down. It was covered in mud and needed quite a lot of pressure on the water-pump to shift it all off.

I glanced around, occasionally, to see if the driver of the tank had appeared but, no, there was no sign of him and its engine was still ticking away merrily. What a waste of gas, I thought, and not only that, the rich exhaust fumes were nearly choking me!

I noticed the Orderly Officer's jeep was still there and, as twenty minutes or so had passed by now, I thought he couldn't possibly have gone to the toilet. He wouldn't be in there all that time, unless he and the tank driver were both in there playing craps!

I finished hosing off the car and put away all the hosepipe gear. I chamoised the car all over and it really looked a treat. The Colonel liked a clean car inside and out, and when I got back to the Motor Pool I would finish off these odd jobs.

I gazed around the park and washrack and still there was no sign of Major Allen, or the tank driver. On the far side of the park a few GIs were doing odd jobs. I clambered up the front of the tank and stood up on the turret. I looked down and could see no-one about. I had never driven a Stuart light tank, so now here's my change to have a go!

I lowered myself down, feet first, through the driver's hatch and as I slumped into the driver's seat, I pressed the gas pedal, accidentally (the stupid guy who had left the tank with the engine running had left the automatic gearbox engaged in drive, with only the park brave lever on) and as I pressed the gas pedal to the floor, the engines roared, the front of the tank reared up, and the tank charged the few feet forward and smashed, with an almighty roar, into the side of the gents latrine, before stalling the engines!

The Disorderly Latrine.

The one-piece solid slab concrete roof came partly down onto the front end of the tank and, with dust and bricks falling everywhere, I could see I could not get out the way I came in, so I scrambled back through and up to the turret exit, banging my head on the breach block of the 37mm gun. I reached up and, after a short struggle, opened the commander's hatch and, behold, a scene of utter destruction lay before me!

God! What have I done! I thought and, in panic, I scrambled off the turret and jumped down. The thick dust was everywhere! Christ! I'll get the sack for sure this time, I thought, and Dad will get drummed out of the Depot!

Suddenly, out of the debris and the clouds of dust, came a dishevelled figure who, momentarily, reminded me of Charles Laughton in shock! His trousers were halfway up his legs and it looked like his arse had been pebble-dashed with the backlash from the toilet!

I couldn't believe my eyes! It wasn't him! Was it? Yes, it was! None other than the Orderly Officer, Major Allen himself, in all his glory! It was then he spotted me!

"I'll kill you, you son-of-a-bitch, you goddam Limey!" he screamed, as he pulled his trousers up and got a real handful of his own muck all over his hands! I can still picture him to this day, shaking it off his hands and half of it splashing on his chin!

He stumbled over the rubble towards me and, as he reached out to grab a yard brush, his trousers fell down again and he fell flat on his face!

A few soldiers were running to help him and, as I sprinted for the Chrysler, the last words I heard were: "Arrest that guy! Shoot the bastard!"

All in one movement, I was in the Chrysler, reversed out and, foot hard down, tyres squealing, I was away!

I knew that I was in real trouble now, but the best thing, I thought, was to go back to me Motor Pool and own up to Dad first, tell him it was nothing but an accident, and await the storm that was sure to come!

I glided into the park at the Pool and stopped in front of Dad's office. I went right in and told him the whole story. I remember Dad's mouth gradually opening wider in disbelief and then he just said: "Wait here, you silly sod!" and he ran out, jumped into the nearest jeep and high-tailed down the road. It appears, he arrived at the washrack just as the Orderly Officer of the Day had, finally, sorted himself out and was about to go and have a shower, then report to the Colonel. Dad tried hard to pacify him, no doubt telling him all sorts of reasons why I did these silly things, but to no avail!

"If your goddam boy apologised a hundred times, it makes no difference whatever. Just look at me! Plastered in shit, and you ask me to forget it! Not on your English fanny!"

Dad arrived back at the office after half an hour, or so, and took the wind right out of my sails, starting on me full throttle!

"Neither I, nor Colonel Richland, or the bloody President can stop you from being sacked, Jim. You have picked on the wrong bloke this time and he'll have your guts for garters, just wait and see!"

I told him I didn't intend to 'wait and see' and I'd strike while the iron was still hot, and go down and ask to see the Colonel to explain to him the whole story. He would like that, I thought. Colonel Richland, who I knew very well by now, was extremely fair, so it was better that I got my say in first!

I ran all the way down to Headquarters, hoping that the Colonel would be in and could see me before he got the full report from Major Allen. I stopped in the corridor outside the office, combed my hair back tidily and knocked on his secretary's door. I could hear light footsteps approaching,

141

then his secretary opened the door. She smiled at me as I asked to see the Colonel on very urgent business.

"I doubt if that's possible," she answered, "as he's in a meeting, and should be at least another fifteen minutes."

"I'll wait, miss," I said, "as it's most urgent."

"Sit down here," she indicated a seat near her desk and I thanked her for her kindness.

I picked up a copy of the *Stars and Stripes* paper and made out I was reading but really my mind was whirling over at top speed, thinking what I was going to say to the Colonel.

Suddenly, the Colonel's office door opened and out trooped two high-ranking officers, leaving the Colonel, apparently, alone at his desk. Eileen, his secretary, walked past me and whispered, "I'll try and arrange for you to see him now, but I won't promise!

In she went and I was straining to her what she was saying, but all I could make out was the Colonel's voice mumbling: "Well, if it won't take too long, yes, okay, send him in Eileen."

My heart was thumping as she showed me in. I walked straight up to his desk and stood to attention and waited for him to speak. Colonel Richland looked up at me.

"Now, Jim boy, what is so urgent today that can't wait for the proper appointment?"

"Well, Colonel Sir," I began, "I have to report an accident on the washrack this morning. When I had washed your Chrysler Imperial, see y . . ." His phone rang, like a death knell, and stopped me in mid-sentence!

"Pardon me," he said, crisply, as he picked up the phone, "take that seat. Go ahead, sit down, Jim boy, you haven't wrecked my car have you?"

He answered his phone, looking at his thumb nail as he listened, intently, to the caller. "Yeah, Yeah. As a matter of fact, he's in my office right now. Yeah. Okay. No injuries? Okay, phone me back in an hour." I never knew who he was speaking to. He dropped the phone, with a crack, on its cradle and looked back at me and said: "Whatever your story is, Jim boy, it sure as hell had better be good. Now, start from the beginning!"

I fired away, and recounted the whole story of what had happened. When I got to the part where the Orderly Officer of the Day came running out of the ruins, he interrupted – "Did you damage my Chrysler?"

"Oh, no, Colonel Sir!"

"What in the hell were you poking about in that tank for? Where was the driver?"

"Dunno Sir – Colonel Sir."

"Have you told your old man?"

"Yes, Colonel Sir."

"I see," he said, and sat back in his chair and studied me intently. "Well, I'll have to await full reports and I will send for you in a few days, but if I were you I would look for another job. Okay?"

I knew that if I left his office now it would be the last time I would see him, so I stalled for time, which was fast running out!

"If I might just say a few more words to you Colonel," – I pressed on, "you see, I only meant to switch the engines off in that tank, they were running for nearly thirty minutes, and to help save gas I only wanted to stop the engines!"

"You telling me that you saw no sign of the driver?"

"No, Sir – I mean Colonel Sir. I couldn't drive away and leave the tank engines running!" I was trying to, slowly, shift the blame onto the absent tank driver! "How about if I help pay for the damage and apologise to the Major personally?" The Colonel flung up his arms in a sign of desperation!

"Jim Boy, let me explain something to you which you do not seem to understand. An officer in the U.S. Army, or anywhere else for that matter, costs thousands of dollars to train. Tanks cost thousands of dollars, and you just go around and continuously smash up the property of the U.S. Army and try to wipe out their officers . . ." I knew he was softening and thought the longer I could drag out the conversation the better it would be for me!

"Colonel Sir, I love the U.S. Army. I love America. (I forgot I'd never been there.) All the things you do in this war are spot on and Bristol-fashion!"

"What's that mean? Bristol-fashion?" he asked.

I explained to him, embroidering a lot, and he nodded. He got out of his large chair and started to walk up and down his office, reading me the riot act, and I knew that, whilst he was rollicking me, he would slowly cool down!

"Oh, and by the way," he continued, "while you are here, what's the story on this I hear from Lieutenant Cohen, who tells me you have actually seen ghosts? Is that true? Do you believe in ghosts?"

"Yes, I do Colonel Sir. I have seen many ghosts! Well, at least three on separate occasions."

"Recently?"

"Yes Sir!"

"Where's that?"

"Well, one's called the Lady of the Lawn, and as I was riding my bike home from Chute one night, a few weeks ago, I passed the haunted house, and a lady in white walked across the road in front of me and went straight onto a lawn on the other side, and just vanished!" I recounted several other stories to the Colonel, adding my own extra bits on the way, and he just stood there speechless! I told him of the lady in the milk float who just disappeared down a well, pony included, and he just repeated over and over – "You don't say!"

"Yes, Colonel Sir, that was on the way to Shoddesdon."

It so happened, the Colonel was very interested in ghosts and, as I sat there recounting my experiences with them, his attitude changed towards me. He asked me if I had seen any ghosts in the old English manors, or the like, and I recounted an encounter I had one evening only a few months previously. He sat down again.

"I was riding my bicycle through the grounds of Biddesden House from the main gates, round the right side of the house, to the rear, as a short cut to get me on the Chute road, to go and meet a girlfriend. As I cycled past the house, there was a large long lawn, and at the back, in the trees, there appeared to be an entrance to a family vault, with old iron gates with some kind of granite stone works. I saw the figure of a lady to my right, and automatically stopped my bike, froze, and the top of my head tingled and it felt as if my hair was standing on end! There she was! Walking slowly towards the vault entrance! I could not quite describe the colour of her lovely long lace-like dress, but it seemed a blue-ish grey. She did not look in my direction, but appeared to be gazing at the lawn, deep in thought. As she walked onwards to the iron gate I did particularly notice what appeared to be a large ear-ring in her ear, which looked – from the distance of ten feet or so – in the bright moonlight, like a bunch of tiny grapes, the colour of pearls. Her hair seemed, not grey, but more like shades of black, worn in plaits, but then tied over her ears, round her head. On reaching the iron gates, she then just walked through and faded out of my vision. I climbed on my bike and pedalled like hell, back home again!"

Colonel Richland sat there, occasionally tapping his cigar ash in the try on his desk.

"Christ, Jim Boy! You've really seen a lot of ghosts. I've never seen any at all. Do you think it possible that you might try to find out from that family who live there if they know who that ghost might be and, if so, the year that she was in residence there, that's if she ever lived there!"

"Yes, Colonel Sir!"

"By-the-way, no need to call me 'Colonel Sir' all the time, just 'Sir' is sufficient, you understand?"

"Yes, Sir!"

The Colonel got to his feet again, walked to the office window, looked out briefly and returned to his large chair and sat down and lit a fresh cigar. He watched the smoke curl up to the ceiling as he said quietly to me, "You know, Jim Boy, I shouldn't say this, but you are really some guy! Everyone I've spoken to thinks you're a swell guy, and you're a good worker, but the goddam tricks you get up to leave me stone cold! When you were in that plane, where the hell did you think you were actually going to end up? How about if you had, by chance, crossed the Channel to France, and the Germans had shot you down. What then?"

"Well, Sir, I hadn't any guns on board, and I wouldn't have flown over there unless I had!"

"Have you got guns someplace, then, Jim Boy?" he asked, giving me a sly look!

"Oh, no Sir. I'm not old enough to have a licence!"

"That's a lot of horse-shit! now, isn't it? You took off in that Piper Cub without one, so why do you suddenly need licences?"

"I don't want to break the law any more, Sir. I feel I would be letting you down if I did, and you have been so good to me. The U.S. Army uniform is beautifully tailored isn't it, Sir? It really does look smart, especially the officers' uniform. I like the pleats you have pressed in the back of your tunic!" The Colonel stood up, walked over to his reflection in the window and looked back over his shoulder at his own neat presses.

"You like that styling, Jim Boy? Haven't you ever seen that before?"

"No Sir, but I'll have my new suit designed like that when I get it!"

The Colonel returned to his desk, sat down and smiled over at me. He slid open a drawer and took out a carton of Chesterfield cigarettes and put them in a paper bag, together with some candy and gum.

"Take these. Don't tell your Dad I gave you the carton, and stay out of trouble, for Christ sake. Let me know if you find out anything about the ghost we've been speaking about, and don't aggravate these English bobbies in the Depot. Okay? Now get on back to your Dad at the Motor Pool!"

I left his office on a cloud. I couldn't believe it, reprieved again! He's a phantomologist – silly big sod!

I didn't hear another word about Major Allen and his disorderly latrine! He got himself posted to another part, which was fortunate for all concerned!

CHAPTER 25

Where's My Harley Davidson?

MONG the equipment supplied to the U.S. Army was a large, very smart, motorcycle, manufactured by Harley Davidson of Milwaukee, Wisconsin, USA. It was coded the WLC model, powered by a V-twin, side valve, 750cc engine. It usually had a large 'buddy-seat' (so called because you could sit your buddy behind you too) and was fitted with large handlebars. This bike was my favourite. I always imagined myself riding one along Fifth Avenue with siren screaming, like their cops did, chasing the gangsters! Now there were quite a few of these 'Harleys' in the Motor Pool but, as yet, I had only a few goes on one, mainly because most of the time they were being used!

Master Sergeant Hoffman was a Military Policeman. He used to be based at the Depot and would ride around, with his sidekick, out into the local countryside and terrorise the GIs who, usually, used to shrink at the sight of them. Wherever there was trouble, M/Sgt Hoffman and company were there, taking down the details.

He took great pride in his Harley. It was always bulled-up. Flashing lights, sirens, the lot! By nature M/Sgt Hoffman was of a nasty disposition. He would put his bike on the lean-to stand at the crossroads in Tidworth at the bottom of Station Road, and just pray all day that trouble would come his way, in big helpings! His ample belly sagged over his immaculate white 'blancoed' belt on which hung a large, heavy, holstered ·45 calibre automatic, and from under his shining white helmet bulged his ears, which looked like two big cauliflowers! His nose, well, it just acted as a fender, or bumper, for the Harley. Aside from that, he wasn't a bad-looking bloke!

He used to park his bike in the Motor Pool and chain it up when he went on furlough. One day he went off for a three-day leave. He never, ever, let anyone ride his bike, "anyway," he said, "no-one else could ride the goddam thing!" So, with his chain and padlock safely on, he would say a few words to it, like "see you in a few days, honey!" and away on leave he went!

He didn't notice me watching all this going on from behind the stores, and the next day, at lunchtime, I planned to pinch it and go over the Downs on the assault course but, as I couldn't ride it out of the main gate, I would have to enrol the help of an accomplice in the person of a certain Private First Class Kelly.

Kelly, as we called him, had been booked many a time by Hoffman and, whilst of lot of GIs wanted the pleasure of smashing his bike up, they hinted that I was best qualified to do the honours, so they would help me to get it out the main gate!

Sergeant Hoffman on his Harley.

The next day, near lunchtime, Kelly got a Studebaker 6 x 6 truck, with a full canvas tilt and, after some trouble cutting through the padlocks on the bike, we pushed the Harley up some ramps into the truck and dropped the back sheets, and away we went, out of the Depot and out onto the assault course – to assault the Harley!

We left the main Tidworth/Everleigh Road and took the rough track that led away into the rough country. On the way it was so bumpy that the Harley fell over on its side and Kelly was laughing, hysterically, all the time. We had to pull up somewhere where we could slide the ramp down against a small bank to run her out easily.

The weather was foul, the rain falling in torrents. We eventually managed to get the bike out and I started her up! Kelly seemed to be getting extremely excited. Then he goes to the truck and fetches a trenching spade and starts lashing out at the front of the Harley, first the windshield went flying!

"Hang on!" I shouted. "Watch out where you swing that bloody thing! I can't dump it out there if you wreck it!"

"All right!" he said, "but I want to piss all over it first!"

"Not with me sitting on it, mate," I shouted, over the noise of the motor and, with that, I dipped the foot clutch, shoved her in first and took off like a bat out of hell!

I headed out to the main course, which was hilly, and in the dips it was very muddy. I knew that I was not going to get far in this weather and soon I could not make hardly any headway at all!

As I got over the next hill, down below me, some fifty feet, was a great flood of water, but it was too late! No way could I stop now! So, thinking discretion was the better part of valour, I jumped off sideways, fast, and let the Harley go alone on her death ride!

In she went, slithered to a stop and fell on her side, then, after a few minutes, disappeared from view! I heard footsteps sloshing up behind me and standing on the top was PFC Kelly, hands to his mouth, imitating the *Last Post*!

Christ, I thought, he's further gone than me! He's definitely bonkers! I sat there covered in mud. I couldn't get up for laughing!

Drenched to the bone, I marched back to the truck, with Kelly bringing up the rear singing, to the tune of *John Brown's Body*: "M/Sgt Hoffman's got some water in his tank, and he won't flag me down anymore, Glory, Glory Hallelujah, Glory, Glory Hallelujah . . ."

He climbed aboard the Studebaker and drove back to the Depot, sneaked in the back way and cleaned ourselves up in the washrooms. I took off most of my clothes and put on some fresh overalls. We were late, and it was just as well Dad was not about, otherwise he would have played hell!

A few days later, M/Sgt Hoffman returned back from his leave. I could see him through the window of the staffroom that morning, sitting with his feet up on the table, drinking his coffee. I could hear his loud voice, as usual, bragging about the conquests he had made with the broads down in London. He had not yet called up by the Motor Pool garage across the road, where he expected to find his Harley still chained up to the wall, where now there was an empty space!

I went back to the garage and awaited his arrival and could not wait to see the look on his face when he found his bike missing.

There was not long to wait as very soon Hoffman came striding into the garage. I had my head under the hood of a jeep, pretending that I was busy. I watched his face as he realised his bike was not in its usual place.

"Where's my Harley Davidson?" he yelled, looking all around the garage. He finally rested his gaze on me.

"Jim, you seen it?"

"No," I replied.

"What d'ya mean, no! You are here working in the goddam place all day. Ainchya?"

"So what? Am I supposed to sit here watching to see if your bike ain't pinched? Anyway, who would want to take that heap?" M/Sgt Hoffman looked at me disdainfully: "I'll tell you who would. A lot of these creeps that ain't got nuthin better to do! Well, I'll find the son-of-a-bitch, don't worry! I'll have whoever it is court-martialled, that's for sure!"

He was walking around in circles, swearing and calling everyone thieving bastards, and was holding the chain up in his hand.

"Look at this!" he was shouting, "they've cut this chain too! There's some jerk, some smart arse, who's gonna be in the stockade by tonight!"

"Oh, stop your bitching, Hoffman!" I shouted, "all this bloody song and dance over a motorcycle! Go and draw a new one!"

"I signed for that son-of-a-bitch," shouted Hoffman, "I'm going to have to explain to the Colonel. Ain't I?"

"So what?" I replied, "you scared to tell him. He won't bite your head of will he? Just tell him the thing has been stolen, and that's that! Let's be honest, Hoffman," I went on, "you ain't exactly very popular round here, are you? I mean, you go around on your Harley, giving everyone in sight a ticket for the most stupid reasons. I mean, I work here all day and here the GIs bitching about it all the time, don't I? And, another thing, I am not here at night or weekends, am I? So, anyone can help themselves to anything they fancy, and it's plain as day, someone has fancied your Harley, haven't they?"

Hoffman sat down on a spare truck wheel which was leaning against the wall.

"Now look, Jim," he said, looking around furtively, "I'll tell you what I'm going to do." He lowered his voice and leaned towards me, "I'll tell you this, in strictest confidence. If you tell me who took my bike, or where I might find it, I'll give you two cartons of Chesterfields!"

"I've told you already. I don't know where the hell it is. Anyway, I don't like those fags!" Hoffman pressed on:

149

"I'll give you any brand you want, and on top of that, I'll give you fifty bucks too! Now, how's that for a real offer?" I tried to stare Hoffman in the eye, without blinking.

"Look, Hoffman. I can't tell you what I don't know, can I? Your best plan is what I've said before. Go and report it and you'll get a new bike. One thing's sure, you're not going to get the other back, are you?"

"No, I guess not!" he replied. "But I got my own inquiries to make yet!" With that, Hoffman, went off, slamming the door as he left!

Two days later, he had a new model and was soon back to his old tricks, giving everyone tickets and a hard time, as before!

Dad asked me a few times about it, but after a few weeks the whole thing seemed to have passed into history!

Early one morning, a farmer was walking down a country lane near Tidworth and found M/Sgt Hoffman lying, severely injured just inside one of his fields. He still wore his white 'snowdrop' helmet and he was rushed to the military hospital in Tidworth.

The full story later came to light. Apparently, Hoffman was chasing a GI in a jeep in the early hours of the morning, on his motorcycle. The jeep was suspected of carrying some black market goods and, in this high-speed chase along the narrow country lanes, Hoffman lost control of his machine on a sharp bend, skidded and crashed through a hedge, throwing him into the field, badly hurt. His ·45 calibre Browning automatic was missing, together with the white lanyard, but more mysterious was the disappearance of his Harley. Not a trace could be found, only a few fragments of glass and odd debris were scattered among the long grass.

Sadly M/Sgt Hoffman, Military Police, U.S.Army, died three days after the accident. He managed to give some details of his crash, but the occupant of the jeep he was chasing was never traced.

Despite his many faults, Hoffman died serving his country and in the line of duty. And, who knows, perhaps he still rides his Harley in his own Valhalla!

CHAPTER 26

A Sherman Called Herman

I HAD seen a lot of tanks before the U.S. Army came, but that had been before the war started. I remember in 1938 John and I used to go to the entrance of a REME Depot, just a small workshop, past Simmonds Road on the way to Brimstone Bottom. Standing on the waste ground was a Vickers medium tank of about 1930 design. It had been parked there for some time, very rusty and quite obsolete, but it seemed to be complete. It even had its 47mm gun still in position in the turret and I used to sit up there and crank the turret around, and aim the gun at some imaginary target over on Windmill Hill in the distance. This was always great fun. If you wound the handle the large armoured turret would creak all the way round and another small handle would elevate, or lower, the large gun. To think one could sit inside this box of steel and lob bloody great shells at the Gerries and be safe inside, that's what it felt like, but I don't think the Royal Armoured Corps held the same view!

In truth, the British Army did not have a worthy tank to face the Germans with when war eventually came in 1939, only one year later. It was also true that in the same year the U.S. Army were even worse off, and when they came into the war in 1941 they had to start from scratch and came up with a couple of new designs, one of these being the Sherman. They were faced with an additional problem when they found they didn't have a suitable engine for it! Eventually, someone realised that stored away in some obscure place were several thousand aero-engines, petrol operated, on high octane aviation fuel. These engines were, by their nature of design, very bulky and needed a rather large compartment to house them, consequently, the Sherman was high in silhouette, and made an easy target for enemy gunners, and the high octane fuel made it a very dangerous residence for the crew when hit by explosives. Its saving grace, however, was its 76mm gun, which gave it a very good chance against the 88mm German gun if it could sneak up fairly close, which was not easy. However, the general train of thought, at that time, was that if they made enough of them, they would probably smother the enemy force, which they did later in the war!

The British Army (just before D-Day) fitted their 17-pounder gun into some Shermans supplied to their tank regiments, renamed Fireflies, this

151

gun really gave the Panzers a lot of problems. It was simply a very deadly piece of artillery, but let's return to the story!

Collingbourne Woods was very large, so should have been called a forest, as it reached from Ludgershall way up to Chute. At that end the U.S. Army converted the area to a training ground for their infantry regiments and, therefore, had earth-moving equipment to contour the ground to look like a real battleground with trenches and barricades. All this training was to help prepare them for D-Day but, on weekends, the GIs took a break and all was quiet until the following Monday when all hell would break loose again.

My brother, John, had rented a plot of land, about ten acres, close to this particular area. He had a few pigs and poultry and used to make money selling eggs, and the odd pig, to the local butcher. He was very secretive about these nefarious activities and it was some time before I found out what he got up to on the edge of Collingbourne Woods. He worked a few hours part-time at Mr Hall's farm at Biddesden, and always came home smelling of manure! John would always lend a few shillings, keeping a record of all transactions in a notebook! Needless to say, there was always an argument as to how much one owned on the promised day, as John tended to tack a bit extra on the loan!

There is something compelling about a tank! You sit in the driver's seat and feel as if you can take on a whole Panzer division!

Now, if you want to get from A to B in a hurry, a Sherman tank is your best bet. No-one will get in your way, even walls and trees will bow to your superiority, and there were hundreds, yes, hundreds of these monsters lined up on the Downs of Salisbury Plain, just ready for the picking, that is if you could sneak past the sentries, get in and start one up, and then be able to get the hell away with it, foot hard down!

The model in question was a twenty-nine-tonner, armed with a seventy-six millimetre gun and, being one of the earlier models, it was powered by a Wright Cyclone nine-cylinder radial air-cooled engine. I planned to 'borrow' one for the weekend, or maybe longer!

There were a few problems connected with this Sherman. One was starting her up from cold, it was rather a long-winded and noisy operation. The engine had to be hand-cranked with a four-foot handle, through a low-gearing, for at least thirty revolutions, to break the oil seal in the cylinders as, being a radial engine, the oil tended to creep past the pistons in the inverted cylinders and would cause damage if not cleared before using the self-starter. When this handle was being cranked it would make a very loud clicking sound, and would alert all the sentries in the area! Furthermore, when that engine started, it had a nasty habit of backfiring until it was well and truly warmed up! One man could manage this whole operation on his own, if need be, but in this case I had to do it all on my own, so this would take one heck of a lot of working out. Was it worth it, anyway?

Herman the Sherman.

Very close to one end of the tank park was a railway, which was usually busy with goods trains pulling army stores up through Ludgershall to Tidworth, and the clatter they made, as they passed with long lines of wagons, would cover up a lot of the noise the tank engine would make. I looked down to the far end of the field, towards Brimstone Bottom, where I could see Frank Gamble out in his front garden. I had worked on these Shermans for a while in the Depot, so I knew how to start them up and drive them, but I had never driven one outside the

Depot, and wanted to go out over the Downs on my own to try climbing the very steep inclines and down the big dips, like being on a roller coaster, and if I could get out on the firing range with a few shells I could have a pot-shot or two at the derelict tanks they used for target practice!

I could, probably, hide this Sherman in Collingbourne Woods and just use it weekends or, if we were invaded, use it as a mobile headquarters for hit and run raids on the invading Germans! Yes, There were great possibilities here and I would have to organise a secret fuel-dump and store some fuel for the engine.

As the goods train never ran to any time-schedule, I had to sit it out late one evening and, after selecting a Sherman on the end of a long line, I checked the fuel gauges and waited for the distant clatter of the goods train, which may not be too long in coming. At least a mile away, I could see two sentries loafing against a tank at the far end of the tank park and it was just beginning to get dark.

If I could pull this off I had to go like the clappers down the hillside,

Jim did NOT 'give way' when he belted across this main Ludgershall-Tidworth road after stealing the Sherman tank heading up to Windmill Hill in 1943. (Photo: Courtesy Frank Gamble, 1994)

154

cross the main road, past Frank Gamble's house at Brimstone Bottom, and up under the bridge by Bridgeman's farm. Then, across the empty camp on the Ludgershall side of Windmill Hill, and across the Everleigh/Collingbourne Ducis Road, then across several ploughed fields, into one corner of Collingbourne Woods, which was many miles long and deep and I knew nearly every square-foot of it!

I pulled the long crank-handle from its bracket on the back of the Sherman and inserted it into position, ready for cranking over. I started to count, winding the handle slowly, just within my reach. Seventeen, eighteen, nineteen, not many more now, I thought, and that infernal clicking noise but, sod it, if I can crank up before the train comes along I can sit in the Sherman and wait and hope for the best!

I clambered into the driver's seat and glanced over the dashboard, checking the left and right and magneto switches, starter and booster switches, Ki-gas direct injection primer pump, ignition switch and so on. I jacked up the seat, so that I was in a good position and checked the fuel levels again. Just under half full on left tank. That would be plenty to get me to the woods easily, as the distance was only about three or four miles across country. I put on the driver's tank helmet and, suddenly, there it was in the distance, the goods train was approaching, puffing away up the slight incline from Ludgershall.

I'll wait until it crosses the little steel bridge and then the noise will be a lot louder. I pumped the Ki-gas four or five times and turned on the left magneto and the ignition. The noise from the train was very loud now, so I pressed the booster switch and starter switch together and the engine spun over. I opened the throttle a bit, but no response! I released the starter and pumped the Ki-gas three more times. I've got to move it, I thought desperately, or else the bloody train will have gone by!

I pressed the booster and starter switch together again and, after a few revolutions, away she fired with an almighty roar, backfiring and spluttering! I switched over to both magnetos and the engine picked up and took on a more even note. I warmed the engine for a few moments.

Right, here goes! I pressed the clutch. Christ, it was heavy! Then I rammed in first gear, revved up, and away she charged, down the slope, like a bull! I changed into second and gathered a little speed, about fifteen miles an hour. I had to go carefully, as it was nearly dark. I headed straight for the main road near Tidworth Down Senior School, up to Bridgeman's Farm.

To steer a Sherman was a feat on its own. There were two long levers and they took some pulling back, but I had lots of practice on these in the Depot tank shop, so I was gone with the wind!

155

I had to turn the lights on as I crossed over the campsite on Windmill Hill and kept up the best speed I could. The sooner I got to Collingbourne Woods and hid this giant the better. Fortunately, I never saw a soul all the way down and I must have been lucky to get away from the tank park without being spotted.

I drove past Sheppard's Farm and on round the far end and short-cut up the centre of the wood, where I knew it was very dense with undergrowth, and charged into the centre, smashing a few trees down, then stopped and switched off the engine.

It was very late. I locked the brakes and climbed out and sat on the turret. My hand rested on the barrel of the seventy-six. Gosh! That was some piece of artillery! I imagined I was just inside the German lines and climbed into the turret and switched on the interior lamps. I turned on the master switch and sat in the gunner's seat, grabbed the pistol-grip, which swivelled left or right, and tilted up and down. This elevated the gun and rotated the turret in whichever direction required. Underneath was the trigger, which fired the gun. I swung the turret to the right. CRASH! – I had forgotten I was among the trees and the gun barrel had smashed against a tree! Oh, sod it! I'll wait till tomorrow, I thought. I brought the gun back to the central position and switched everything off, climbed down from the tank and legged it home.

My Dad was waiting up for me this time and gave me a smack round the ear for being late home! I was sent to bed with no supper, which was only a slice of bread with lard on, anyway, so I didn't miss much! I jumped into bed and was laying there, planning the manoeuvres for the next day. I had to think of a name for the Sherman. It was fat and ugly, so I decided to call it Herman, after that fat slob Goering and so, tomorrow, I would pee all up the side of it and christen it Herman!

The next day dawn warm and sunny. It will be most important, I thought, to get down early and get Herman parked deeper into Collingbourne Woods and completely camouflaged!

One problem would be getting high-octane fuel and transporting it to a secret cache near Herman, so I would have a good supply close at hand if I ever had to chase any Gerries! If they invade us, I would have enough fuel for a few 'recces' into their lines. I just had to get some seventy-six millimetre shells in the very near future, as a gun without ammo was useless, even though, at worst, I could run over a few buggers! Mind you, there was a thirty-calibre machine gun fixed parallel to the seventy-six and another at the front, next to the driver, but I had to obtain at least thirty shells. That would kit us out right.

I left home at 8.00 a.m. You just couldn't believe there was a war on and that only sixty-odd miles away in France the Germans were there, trying at every opportunity to kill us all. I walked on down Crawlboys. I couldn't wait to reach the Sherman and hoped that no-one had heard or seen me park up the night before.

I did a little shadow-boxing as I trotted on – left, left and then an upper-cut, another two straight lefts. Christ, I thought, if that landed on someone's jaw they'd go down like a log. The postman cycled down the hill past me.

"Mind you don't knock yourself out, Jimmy!" he shouted.

Cheeky sod, I thought! Little did he know that I had a Sherman tucked away for an emergency and all he had was a bloody pushbike. Still, he had done his bit in the last war, I thought. Good chap he was, always friendly with everyone, especially me. His name was Ernie Lansley and he definitely was the fastest postman in Wiltshire.

I walked on and into the edge of Collingbourne Woods. I would soon come across the track marks made the night before and, shortly, I was following them deep into the woods. At last, I mused. I've got my own tank!

Herman was only twenty feet away before I could make out the outline of this khaki monster, seemingly crouching among the deep undergrowth, trying to avoid me! I climbed up, pulling myself up from the front, grasping the large gun and barbette and pulled open the hatch and climbed down into the turret. I would have to go through the whole ritual of starting procedures again and start up, move my bivouac, and penetrate deeper into the wood for the permanent camouflage. Soon we would be ready for any eventualities!

I climbed out again to hand-crank the engine over to clear the oil but, first, I had to christen Herman. To make matters worse, I didn't really want a pee! Anyway, I made a supreme effort, strained myself, and peed right up the side! I tried to go up higher but couldn't, so I settled for that and christened Herman good and proper, shouting: "I name you Herman, may God bless her and all who ride in her!" As I stood there holding my 'willie' I had a strong feeling that someone was watching me. I looked around, staring hard, trying to penetrate the dense foliage. Then, John popped his head up!

"So, that's what you're up to, you crafty sod! Who are you talking to?" He had seen me sneak out and had followed me at a distance, sly bugger was John! "Where did you get that? How long has that been there? Give us a ride!"

"You never came up and gave me a hand to pinch it and now you want jam on it!" I retorted.

"You never asked me, did you?"

John walked up to Herman. He was dressed in khaki breeches and gaiters and U.S. Army boots dyed black, his ruddy face in contrast to his blond hair. He was, basically, of a quiet temperament, but a tough handful when you riled him, so it was better not to upset him! He kicked the bogey-wheel on Herman.

"Bloody lot of scrap, this!" he jeered, walking right round the Sherman, eyeing it up and down and whistling quietly. It seemed he was the only person I knew who could whistle without, apparently, opening his mouth!

"I bet a bulldozer is tougher than this!" he retorted.

"What do you mean?" I queried.

"I've got a giant bulldozer!" he sneered, still walking round Herman and giving it the odd kick!

"Stop kicking the bloody thing!" I shouted. I was beginning to get annoyed!

"Oh, dear me! Are you afraid it'll fall to bits, then?" he sneered.

I wanted to kick him straight up the arse and it was then he said. "Don't you want to see my bulldozer, then, Jim?"

"See your bloody bulldozer? That's a load of bull! Where is it then? In your dreams, you silly sod!"

John bent down and pulled up a dry blade of grass and pushed it between his two top front teeth. His teeth ain't as good as mine, I thought!

"If you give us a ride in that, I'll show you where it is!" he said. My curiosity was getting the better of me. Did he really have a bulldozer?

"All right. How far is it then?" I asked.

"About a mile up, near the pond, and I bet you its engine is more powerful than yours!" he indicated the Sherman scathingly.

"Look, mate," I said, "nothing is stronger than Herman, so show me where it is. Get on board and sit in the turret and don't touch anything while I start her up!"

I went through the whole starting procedure and jumped down and sat in the driver's seat, telling John to sit alongside me.

"Unclip your hatch, push it up and over until it clicks and locks open, and don't bang your head!" He stepped down from the turret platform and gazed at the huge breech on the 76mm gun.

"I bags first shot with this!" he shouted.

"Wind that seat up so your head is just peeping out of the top and watch out for branches as we go through the bushes!"

JIM STOODLEY'S PRIVATE WAR

I started her up after the second attempt and warmed the engine for a few minutes. I gunned the engine a few times. I loved to see the rev-counter bounce up and down.

John sat there and bent down shouting "Let's go, Jim. Into battle – forward!"

"Shut up, you daft sod and just keep your eyes open in front of you!"

I put the helmet on. It was too big, but it would protect my head a bit. I shoved in first gear and off we went. I regained the path that led up to the pond. The roar of the engine was terrific and the draught was blowing dust into my eyes, so I stopped with a lurch and tapped John on the arm. He climbed over to me and I shouted into his ear "Close that turret hatch! Press the clip back and slam the sodden thing!"

He went back up into the turret and fiddled around for several minutes until I heard the lid drop with a clang. John came back down and took his seat. The draught had stopped and off we went again! After fifteen minutes, or so, we reached the pond. It was about forty feet across and about three feet deep. We had, in the past, used a raft made of oil drums and floated over it, but today we weren't going to float over, we'd go through it!

I swung around to the left a little and lined up, charging the pond. Down the slight bank and in we went, ploughing water up over the front and right over my head. I instinctively lowered my head as we drove through and up the other side. Water was running in down my legs and inside my collar. I pulled up and stopped once we had gained the level ground and switched off the engine, then we both climbed out. Steam was hissing from the exhaust pipes and the pond seemed half empty after we had splashed half the water out onto the banks!

"How about going back through again, Jim?" John was enjoying this! "Have you got any ammo? We can . . ."

"Where's this bulldozer you said you had?" I interrupted.

"Follow me," he said, and I did.

We walked for a minute or two, turning this way and that, until there, down in a drop in the ground, was the biggest Caterpillar bulldozer I had ever set eyes on! The blade on the front was so massive, it had to have a steel boom, with hawser wires, to lift and lower it!

John stood back, hands on hips, swanking over his giant monster. I made out I was not impressed, but I had a job trying to conceal my amazement. I admitted to myself that John had really been telling the truth all along!

John chirped up suddenly, "Got two engines that, you know, a little donkey-engine to start the big one. I've been practising starting it and have been driving it backwards and forwards for a few weekends and, see that pile of earth? I pushed that all the way from down there!" he pointed to the edge of the woods, fifty yards away. The pile of earth was gigantic!

"The Duel" at Wick Pond.

"Yes, I know it has two engines, John. We have some in the Depot and I've had a go on one!" I lied, with a straight face. John went on:

"That 'Cat' would push that all the way to Ludgershall!"

"Don't talk stupid!" I retorted, "you've got no chance against Herman!"

"Who's Herman?" John laughed.

"That's that I've nicknamed him!" I said.

John burst out laughing and, pointing back to where the Sherman stood, shouted: "That wouldn't pull you out of bed!" I was starting to get mad.

"Look," I shouted, "you can't even start the bloody 'Cat', let alone drive it!"

"Can't I? Just watch!" John replied and I sat on the grass and lit up a Lucky Strike and thought "this is going to be funny!"

John walked, cockily, over to where this monster stood. The tracks alone were up to his chin! He climbed up and, after a few minutes, I heard the donkey-engine start. It was revving its head off! Suddenly, the main engine roared into life in a cloud of smoke and I sat there lost for words! John got into the huge seat, which was wide enough for three men! After a lot of grinding and revving, it started to roll towards me. I was up, and off! I looked back and all I could see was a red, laughing face, peering over the blade. First he would swing to the left and then to the right then, suddenly, he just kept going round as if on a sixpence, then it stopped. With the engine ticking over, John jumped down and came running over, still laughing.

"How about that for a bit of smart driving?" he chortled. No fool this one, I thought, but he's too cocky, I'll have to show him some real driving!

"I'll tell you what, Jim. I bet I can push that Sherman backwards, forwards, and any way you like!"

Now, this was my chance to really show him, I thought. I secretly wished I had some armour-piercing shells on board Herman, so that I could blow his 'Cat' to smithereens!

"John, you're all talk!"

"Am I?" he said, "get in that dustbin of yours and let's see who's the toughest! You're the one with all the mouth!"

I ran down to Herman, hopped up and then down inside, started the engine and swung her round and faced the Cat, which was barely visible through the dust as I locked her round on one track! John was already sitting in the Cat and slowly creeping up on me. This is the duel of the monsters, I thought, so I'll show the smart-arse a few tricks!

Now, John, if he found himself losing out, had a tendency to get nasty and cheat, and was not past giving you a sly one with whatever happened to be within his reach, so, with him sitting up on the Cat, I would have to make sure I didn't upset him too much, and would have to keep well clear of that bloody great blade on the front! I'd let him believe he was winning the duel a bit, then give his Cat a good bashing up the back end, then hightail it away. With my superior speed he would have no chance of catching me! I looked down at the fuel gauges, still plenty of gas. I gave the engine a few quick revs.

I was brought back to reality by a terrific smashing sound and a jolt which made me bang my head severely and split my helmet in the process. I had been lowering my seat and adjusting the driver's periscope

161

and had not seen John creeping up on me, smashing the massive 'dozer blade against the front armour of my tank, and pushing the Sherman backwards a few feet, frightening the life out of me!

The dirty swine, I'll wipe the bloody smile off his face! I rammed the gear lever in first and charged forward the few feet, slamming the bulldozer's blade with a horrific crash, and stalled the engine! Blast it! I must start up quickly, I thought, before John lost his rag!

I re-started, selected reverse and roared back blindly, out of harm's way, then, at a safe distance, stopped and started forward again, circling the Cat! As I did so, John was locking one track and skidding around on a sixpence to prevent me whacking him in the backside on the sly!

I decided to charge him blind. I aimed the Sherman at him and put on full throttle, let go of the steering levers and held on for dear life!

John saw my game and shot away and I charged past and just missed him by inches! I roared straight into the pond and stalled the engine again! Of all the places to be stuck in! A three-foot pond!

I started to panic! I could not see what John was up to and that worried me a lot. I tried to open the driver's hatch, but it would not budge, so I scrambled back through and up into the turret and looked out of the top. I was petrified! There was John, charging towards me with the blade of the Cat lowered.

"Stop, you mad sod!" I shouted, but he could not hear me over the noise! I dropped down inside the turret just as he hit me with a loud crunch, right against the side of the tank!

I lay on the floor of the turret, thinking "leave the silly sod alone and he will be bound to get tired and eventually bugger off!" Then suddenly, I felt the floor beneath me rising as he had wedged the big blade against the side under the bogey-wheel, and was lifting and pushing the Sherman up at an angle, a few feet off the ground.

I scrambled back up the best I could to the turret hatch, finding it hard with the angle of the Sherman. I popped out my head and shouted to John, waving him off, but it was no use, he had his motor on full throttle and couldn't hear me anyway. So I decided to 'abandon ship' pronto!

I slithered down the front, splashing away, fast, to the bank, and ran like hell in case the Sherman rolled forward onto me! I'll smash his face in when he gets off that thing, I thought. John than backed the Cat off and stopped the engine and just sat there laughing! I sat down on the bank, my trousers soaking wet and shouted over to him:

"You slimy, cheating sod! You knew my engine had stalled! You should have backed off!

"All's fair in war, mate!" he replied, "anyway, I thought you could drive! You're always bragging how good you are! And look at that load of scrap in the pond! Bloody useless those Shermans. The Churchill tank would make two of that! I sat there seething, planning a way to get even. "You won't run over many Gerries with that, will you, Jim?" he taunted!

I looked across to where the Sherman lay in the water. It did look a sorry sight! I have got to use a bit of tact here, I thought!

"Okay, John. I suppose the Cat is stronger after all, so let's see if you are smart enough to push it out on dry land!"

"All right, but, in future, don't go bragging about that thing, see!"

"Okay, go on, push her out then!" John started the engine and slowly pushed the tank out of the water and up onto the bank.

"There you are mate. How's that?" he smirked, swanking.

I scrambled up on to the front of the tank, climbed inside and, after a while, got the engine re-started again. John, meanwhile, had decided to have a pee and, as soon as he turned his back on me, I put on full throttle and charged him where he stood! I really took him by surprise and he wet all down his leg as he ran away from the monster rumbling after him, starting to run in and out between the small trees to avoid me!

I smashed the trees down as I went after him this way and that. I'll shake the bugger up, I thought, as he swung one way then the other. I just kept on after him. Then, suddenly, he ran around behind me and must have jumped up on the back of the tank, because the next thing I knew, he was standing on the turret behind me shouting "Okay, smart ass! Weren't quick enough were you!"

I give up, I thought. I looked ahead and headed to the pond and down the bank at full speed. As we ploughed through the water he got soaking wet through with the spray! I ploughed on and out on to the dry bank and then stopped the engine and we both climbed down on to the ground, laughing. Here we were, in the middle of Collingbourne Woods in the middle of the war, having the time of our lives!

I looked out across the woods. The sun was shining and the birds were singing. John was trying to dry his face. He was a good sport really, and if you let him have things mostly his own way, he was not too bad! The sun would soon dry out our wet clothes. I kicked off my boots and put them up on the front of the Sherman to dry out. The pond looked a bit low on water after our 'battle'.

I looked across at John. He was picking his nose, which he did a lot when he was thinking. I used to scratch my bum. John would pick his nose, stare at it for a while, then see how far he could flick it! Another habit he had was to cough and fart at the same time, in short controlled bursts! That was really something, and made me jealous! I tried it once and, to my amazement, messed my trousers, so I never tried that one again, as I had to tuck my trouser bottoms into my socks and had to walk stiff-legged until I arrived home. Yes, John was a case. We certainly had some great times together!

I had just about driven every type of U.S. Army vehicle there was to drive and life could not have been more full of adventure! I badly wanted to go to war and fight the Germans. I felt hamstrung. I looked up at the 76mm gun on the Sherman. Boy, I would love to have a go at some Gerries with that thing! John had walked slowly over to the pond and was poking about in the water with a stick.

"Ain't no newts in here now, is there, after the bashing about they had with that tank, Jim? Plenty of tadpoles though! Look at the frog-spawn!" I walked over to where he stood, my clothes now nearly dry. John gave me a fag and I gave him a light.

"Come on, Jim. What are we doing now? I'm hungry. Are we going to have some dinner?"

"Yes," I replied and took a few sandwiches out of my pocket and gave him a couple to get on with.

"Sod them things!" John said. "Get that shovel off the back of the Sherman and let's dig out a rabbit over there," pointing to a cluster of burrows near the trees. "Light a fire and dig one out and we'll have a proper meal!"

I unclipped the shovel and started to dig out a rabbit, not too sure there would be one down the hole. I blocked up the remaining holes and soon I was down a couple of feet and could hear the movement of a rabbit panicking! I dug away, slowly, and soon came upon the rabbit and nearly lost it as it made a dive for freedom. I grabbed it and stretched its neck and gave it to John to skin and clean, ready for cooking over a roaring fire on his home-made spit.

"Going to be a bit of a rough dinner isn't it, John?"

"No, it'll be all right, it's only a small one and should cook through okay!" he replied.

After about an hour, we sat down to a fairly burnt but tasty dinner and all we were short of was a drink, but we would soon have to go home and get ready for tea.

"Let's get the tank back and hide it in the woods till I want to use it again, and you'd better get the Cat back to where you found it, John."

"Yes, I'll put her back and hope the Yanks don't notice it's been used!"

I climbed up on to the Sherman and started it up and moved off, back to my hiding place deep in the woods, pushing small trees down before me as I ploughed on. I finally selected an ideal spot and pulled up and stopped, shut down the motor and climbed down and went back to where John had just finished tidying up is Cat.

"Ready, John?"

"Yes, I'm ready. Let's get going, as it's about an hour's walk home, and if we're late for tea, Dad will start moaning!"

We walked on down through the woods. It was a beautiful afternoon with the sun setting slowly in the west, and here and there a red squirrel scampering up a tree and the birds singing as they flitted through the undergrowth. All this beauty! How lucky we were. Everywhere there seemed to be something to marvel at. We were so lucky to live in this part of the country.

Feeding time was something to look forward to at our house, because, if you looked backwards, your dinner was gone in five seconds flat! We had a very long table in our kitchen, with two wooden benches on either side, and there was usually a rush for the end seat at the top, so you could get a grab at the grub as it arrived in a large bowl which looked like a cut-down oil drum. Mum would fill the plates and we would pass them down the line until it was your turn, and you were also handy to the bowl for a sly extra spoonful when Mum or Dad were not looking!

Mum had a large carving knife and anyone who snatched something out of turn would get a crack across the knuckles, but with practice you could make a dummy run and, as she missed you, if you were smart, an extra bit was yours! If Dad didn't get you from the other end of the table! But Dad was not a bad chap, he would only prong you once with his fork! But getting back to Herman.

I just had to get some fuel for him and get it hidden really deep in the woods at the first chance I got, but for the time being the tank could stay hidden where it was. Soon, perhaps, I could go out for a long-range patrol and when I obtained a few shells for the gun, I could lob a few over to the firing ranges for practice, or mock-attack some of the U.S. Army when they go out in their armoured columns on manoeuvres. It didn't take much to get the Yanks going if they got a ·76mm shell dropped near them, but that will have to wait!

There wasn't much point having a tank without being able to use the advantage you had, and you could not use its artillery. I obtained some U.S. Army rations and stored them in the turret. There was plenty of space here as normally these spaces were used by the shells for the ·76mm gun.

I didn't have much luck with the radio. I did sometimes get some music and, occasionally, other tank commanders talking to each other when they were out on war-games. I had plenty of ·30 calibre ammo for the machine-gun that was fixed in tandem alongside the ·76mm I tied some branches on the outside and this made it very hard to spot, especially from the air. I had lots of practice in the turret, tracking and elevating the gun and firing at imaginary targets.

I made my way back home. There would be other days to spend in Collingbourne Woods!

CHAPTER 27

Meeting the Girls of Leicester Square

EVERY time the Yanks came back from their leave in London, I had the same old stories from them. They were forever bragging about their conquests with this girl or that and these excursions always seemed to start from the area around Leicester Square. It seemed, to me, that this was a bit of a shady place and if one wanted to get acquainted with them, then this was the place to go!

I had not been out with many girls, as I had always seemed to be doing other mischievous things, but I was beginning to feel a little put out by the guys telling me, every Monday morning, about the the goings on in London! It seemed that either the girls down there were man-mad, or that the Yanks were some kind of special Rudolph Valentinos. Anyway, I figured that what they could do I could do better, so I decided to go down to London on the next weekend and give the girls of Leicester Square a visit!

It would be quite a change for the GIs to listen to my yarns on a Monday morning. I would catch an early train from Andover Junction and as the girls charged between three and five quid, according to the Yanks, I would need to take a few quid to see me over the weekend. Then I could hit the town in a big way. I would have to stay out all night again and Dad would moan about that, but it was well worth the earache from him! I had been on the missing list so often, that once more would not matter. Anyway, I just had to go down and find out for myself just what the guys were getting so excited about so that, when I arrived in London dressed to kill in my best suit, the girls would very likely fight over me. I'll show the Yanks! Let me see, I would need some 'french letters', about a dozen would do, seeing I really mean to do things in a big way! Anyway, I gotta be ready for the rush!

It was a lovely morning as I stepped off the train at Waterloo Station. I felt like a million dollars all spruced up in my best gear, as I proceeded to make my way to the taxi stand which the guys had told me about. I strolled up to the nearest one and, as I approached, I noticed the driver eyeing me up and down. I put on the American accent, to try to impress him.

"Say, buddy, take me to where the women are. You get my drift? You know, where the action is! I'm here for a good time, so burn the rubber, man!" The driver turned round, looking at me, a bit startled, and dryly replied:

"The only place I know where there's any action, mate, is over the bloody Channel, and you ain't old enough for that, let alone any bloody girls! You may as well drop the Yankee accent too, and jump out and go back to Mummy!"

Oh, I thought, we've got a smart-ass Cockney here, so I decided on a new tack.

"Okay, mate," I replied, becoming a Limey again, "you can't blame me for trying to get some experience, can you? You were my age once weren't you?"

At this remark the driver seemed to change his stance and said to me: "The first time in London is it? You want to see the lights and get to know the girls, yeah?"

"You're dead right, mate," I replied.

"How old are you?" he went on.

"I'm just sixteen-and-a-half and ready for anything, mate!"

"You don't look sixteen to me!" he retorted.

"I am, and I've heard that the cafe in Leicester Square is the place to pick up the broads!"

"Yes," he answered, "and you can pick up more than that, if you're not careful! I'll drop you off at the Square and you can have your pick of about a thousand tarts, if that's what you are looking for! And the fare will cost you ten bob. All you got to do is to sit in the cafe and, sooner or later, some gal will come and ask you to go along with her! Okay, mate?"

"Okay!" I replied.

Off we drove and, within a few minutes, we were in the Square. I paid him and he drove off, leaving me standing on the pavement like a spare prick! I looked around me. The place was crowded with every nationality of soldiers one could imagine! I was waiting for the rush of girls in my direction but, up to now, there were none! They couldn't have seen me! So I didn't feel too downhearted!

I must have been standing there for at least two hours and, it slowly dawned on me that I wasn't going to be the big hit I thought I was! With my vanity a little dented, I decided to stroll along the street a bit and, hopefully, I may have some luck! I stopped at a large jewellers and looked in the window for a while, weighing up the girls in the reflection from the window, as they passed. After a while, a tramp came strolling up to me and asked me for half-a-crown. "I want to get some grub, mate," he said. I felt rather embarrassed, as I had never had anyone ask me for dough before! I put my hand in my pocket and took out some change, gave him five-bob and off he went, mumbling his thanks, and I watched as he crossed the road and went straight into the pub opposite! The cheeky sod, I thought, he didn't tell me it was a liquid lunch he wanted!

It was just then, that two very smart girls caught my eye. They seemed to be heading my way, ambling along slowly, chatting between themselves. Here's my chance, I thought, and as they drew level with me, I asked them the time.

"Nearly three o'clock, dearie," one replied, "You don't sound like you come from around here!"

"No, I'm from Wiltshire!" I answered. "You've heard of the swede-bashers, you know, the moonrakers! Haven't you?"

"Oh, yes!" replied the red-head. "My name's Cathy and my friend's name is Gloria," she went on, "We're both seventeen. How old are you, and what's your name?"

"My name's Jim and I am seventeen," I lied.

"Is this the first time you've been in London, Jim?" asked Cathy.

"Yes, it is," I replied, as we began to walk, slowly, down the street.

"Would you like us to show you around the sights?" giggled Gloria.

"Yes, that would be nice!" I replied, "where do you suggest?"

Well, there's Hyde Park and Tower Bridge, and all sorts of interesting places. Or, if you like, we can just walk around the shops!"

I began to think. Now, this could turn out to be an expensive afternoon with two of them in tow. There doesn't seem much chance of separating them! I guess I shall just have to play it by ear for a while! I suddenly hit on an idea! I could take them to the movies and ditch them in there and try my luck some place else!

"How about going to the pictures?" I asked. They both looked at each other and nodded in agreement. "Okay!" I said, "Let's go!"

In we went to the Odeon Cinema nearby. I bought three plush seats in the circle, taking care they did not see my wad of notes! We settled down to watch the film, with me sitting in between them, like a squashed prat!

Gloria seemed to be the better of the two. She was very slim and much quieter than Cathy, who was a big girl. And I mean BIG! Towards the end of the show, I glanced at the time, nearly seven o'clock. When the show ended, we all left and stood outside on the pavement. It was dark, and a bit chilly. The girls said they were a big hungry. Christ, I thought, now it's really going to cost me a bomb, but I just can't drop them here. I'll have to give them a feed up! A dear do this is going to be, but, never mind, the night is still young!

"Okay, girls, let's get some eats! We went off in search of a cafe. Many we tried were crowded, but we eventually found a small one off the Square. That took care of three pounds and another two hours and, by now, it was nearly 9.00 p.m. I was beginning to remember what I had really come to London for in the first place, when, suddenly, Cathy – the big one – came straight out with it!

"Ever been with a girl, Jim? You know – been with a girl?" I was taken aback with the direct question and could feel my face going as red as a beetroot!

"Course I have! Loads of times! Why do you ask?" I replied.

"Well, if you like, you can come to our house. You see, Gloria lives with me. My Dad is in the army in the Western Desert and Mum is staying in Glasgow for a week, so, if you'd like to come back to the house you can sleep with both of us. That would be something new for you, wouldn't it, ducks?" I sat there, pondering my reply, already fantasising three in a bed! Maybe it's not such a bad idea, I might get the two for the price of one! Could turn out to be a cheap night after all! And three in a bed! That really tickled my fancy! The GIs would be seething with jealousy when I got back and told them about that one! Perhaps they wouldn't believe me after all the trouble but, never mind, I thought, I'd have a go! I looked up at the girls, who were giggling between themselves.

"Well, how much is this cosy company going to cost then?" I went on, looking as straight as I could at them.

"Oh, only four pounds, all in, if you know what I mean!" Cathy giggled.

"Okay," I replied, "I'm game! Let's go! How far is you home, Cathy?"

"Only five minutes' walk, or so," she replied.

Soon, I found myself walking out of the Square and down several side roads. It was pitch black, as there was a strict black-out in force.

"By the way," piped up Gloria, "Don't be offended, but would you mind paying us now, as we have been let down a couple of times before, by not getting paid!" I saw nothing wrong in that and, after all, I had them hanging on either side of me.

"Yes, sure, I'll pay you now. How much did you say? Four quid?"

"Yes," they answered in unison, "four pounds."

"That's where we live, next house but one," Gloria said, nodding to a house in a long line of terraced houses of which, in the black-out, only a faint outline was visible! I stopped and took out my dough.

"Have either of you girls got change of a five-pound note?"

"No, sorry, we're skint, but I'll go in my house and get the change off my Gran." I gave her the fiver and she walked the few feet down the road to her door.

"I'll go with you," said Cathy, "and go to the toilet while you get change."

I sat down, for a moment, on the low wall and lit a fag, conjuring up all sorts of tricks we were going to get up to all night! In the distance, I could hear the steady hum of the traffic around Leicester Square, but everywhere seemed pitch black and forbidding.

I stubbed out my fag and suddenly realised that the girls had not returned. At least ten minutes had gone by since they went in the front door. I'll give them a couple more minutes, I thought, then I'll give a knock on the door to hurry them up.

After a while, I decided to knock and, after walking up the short flight of steps, gave three sharp taps on the door and waited. No answer! I bent down and pushed open the letter-box flap to shout through and, as I did so, a rush of cold air hit me in the face! That's strange, I thought, her Gran must be living in a bloody morgue! I knocked on the door again, this time much harder and, suddenly, the door opened a few inches on its own. I pushed it fully open and, instead, of looking into the hallway, I could see the stars above and rubble in front of me! All that remained was the complete front shell of the house! The roof and back of the house was just a pile of rubble. It had been blitzed!

Then it dawned on me! 'Jim, Boy, you've been taken on your first ride! Your five is gone, your girls are gone and whatever else there was supposed to go with it!'

I stood there, fuming. 'You bloody fool' I called myself out loud and walked dejectedly back in the general direction of Leicester Square. I'll bloody strangle the pair of them if I meet them again, I thought, as I stumbled along the dark road.

I eventually arrived back at the Square and had already had enough of London. I was quite a few quid down and nothing to show for it, but was reluctant to give in, even though it was getting very late. I walked slowly through the Square and, after about fifteen minutes, a dark-haired young lady, about twenty-years-old, asked me if I was looking for a place for the night.

"Where's your place, then?" I inquired.

"Well, I didn't mean my place, luv, I know a hotel where we can go and stay the night. It's not far, but we will have to get a taxi there."

"Okay," I replied, relieved at last to get fixed up, and asked her to lead the way. She led me up to a line of taxis and, after talking to the driver, whom she appeared to know well, she beckoned to me and I crossed over.

"Here we are," she smiled, "let's jump in this one and we will try that hotel I know of, but you'll have to give the driver ten bob, and I want five quid for the night!"

"Look luv," I replied, "I've already been taken for a ride tonight but, fair dos, here is the ten bob for the driver, and a fiver for you."

She grabbed the money, paid the driver and off we motored. After a few minutes, we stopped outside a small, dingy-looking hotel.

"Hang on, luv," she said, "I'll slip in and see the night-porter and try to get a room."

While I waited in the cab, the driver was telling me what a hot bit of stuff she was and how lucky I was to be staying the night with her. She suddenly re-appeared from the hotel and got into the cab with me.

"Oh dear, what a shame! Just missed the last vacant room!" she told me. "Never mind, I know another place!" and with that, directed the driver to some other hotel. Eventually, we pulled up outside what seemed to be a nice place and I could already imagine myself and my companion sharing one of its plush rooms!

"Look, Jim. It is Jim, isn't it?" she asked.

"Yes," I replied.

"Oh, I'm Nancy, by the way. Look, Jim. You give it a try will you? You look the lucky type!"

"OK," I agreed, and crossed the road and up the steps I went. I went in and up to the little desk where a neat, balding little man with beady eyes watched my approach.

"Yes, Sir, can I help you?" he asked, as he looked me up and down. The time must have been around two in the morning!

"Er – Yes. Have you got a room for the night?" I asked. "It's for me and – my wife!" I felt the colour rise in my cheeks as he stared hard at me.

"No luggage, Sir?"

"Er – no! I'm just on quick visit to London!" (Wants to know a lot, nosey bugger, I thought.)

"Oh Yeah!" replied, "No luggage then, sir," he said, seeming to look at the vacant space around my feet.

"Well, no, just a quick look at the sights. Back to Andover in the morning!" A smile crept to his face.

"Did your wife come with you in that cab?" he asked, craftily.

"Yes," I replied.

"Well, well!" he laughed. "She's just left you!"

"What do you mean?" I asked, alarm in my voice.

"Your bird's just flown! Vanished! Come on, lad, you must be every bit of fourteen! Did you give her any money?"

"Yes," I confessed, realising he knew my game.

"It happens all the time!" he went on. "Mugs like you get caught every night. How much did you give her?"

172

"Five pounds ten shillings!" I replied. By now I had shrunk to three feet tall!

"Well, well!" he said again, "your bird's flown, hasn't she? And to make things worse, sonny, we're full up! If I were you I'd piss off back to Waterloo Station and get the first train out. Have you got any money left?"

"Yes," I replied.

"Look, lad, I'll make you a cup of tea and find out the first train for you. Take a tip from an old hand, stay away from London until you're a lot older, okay?"

"Yes, fine. Thanks very much," I replied, disconsolately. He disappeared for a few minutes and I took a seat by the heater, thinking over the night's happenings, my ego quite deflated!

"Here you are. Get that down you," said the night-porter, as he came back with a mug of tea and a couple of sandwiches.

"Thanks, mate. You are kind, I really appreciate your help!"

"Oh, that's nothing," he replied. "Just put it down to experience, or lack of it, shall we say. By the way, the first train out for Andover is 6.30 a.m. and you have a long wait, haven't you? You don't seem a bad sort of lad, so, if you like, you can have a warm till five-thirty, then I'll get a taxi for you to Waterloo. All right, lad?"

"Yes," I replied. "You're very kind, and I appreciate your help!"

"Think nothing of it," he replied, "I have a lad about your age. I'm sure I wouldn't want to see him stuck in your shoes!"

I must have nodded off for a couple of hours, as I was dead beat, when the porter woke me up saying there was a taxi outside waiting for me.

"Look here," I said to him, "take this money from me as I appreciate your kindness and concern." He pushed my hand away.

"Don't offer me anything, but just promise me you'll stay out of town, and if you must spend any money, then buy your Mum something when you get home. Now, come on, off you go, son, and good luck!" I thanked him and took the cab back to Waterloo. When I arrived there I hung around until the train was boarding and soon I was on my way, back to Andover Town!

There would be no tales to tell the GIs when I arrived back at the Depot on Monday morning, so I guessed I would have to spin them some sort of face-saving yard. If I told them the truth I would be the laughing stock of the Depot. Maybe I had better say nothing at all!

CHAPTER 28

PFC 'Scabby' Norton

I WAS sitting in the drivers' rest room, pondering on a little matter of how to get a few seventy-six millimetre shells for the Sherman I had hid up in Collingbourne Woods. How in hell am I going to get some, I don't know, I thought. That's going to be a tough order, but I was dying to have a go with the bloody great gun on Herman and I had searched all the known ammo dumps in the area, without success! Just then Corporal Topple came in.

"Hi, Jim, goofing off again?"

"Yeah! The same as you, Top. Where have you been?"

"I'm out early in the morning. Just parked my truck up for the night. I gotta go to Southampton tomorrow. Got a load of ammo to drop off at the docks."

"What kind you got on board, Top?"

"Oh, I think a load of ·40mm and some ·76mm and grenades."

"Oh," I replied innocently. I could not believe my ears! I'll have a look later, I thought, and see if there's any cases handy. If there is, I'll whip a few!

Top eventually cleared off to barracks and soon I was up in the back of this truck, and there were the 76s, in their packing cases, at the rear end of the load. Now, how am I going to get a few out of the Depot? That's going to be the problem! Or is it? My eyes wandered over to an ambulance parked nearby. I knew the driver very well and, maybe, I could get him to drop them down near Collingbourne Woods, then I could wheel them up to the tank after dark, on a hand-cart! But, it would have to be tonight, and I would have to go over to the cabin where I would find PFC Scabby Norton, the driver of the ambulance. Everyone called him 'Scabby' because he had a very bad skin, but he didn't seem to mind the nickname at all!

I walked into the cabin, and there was Scabby, asleep as usual, sitting in an old armchair with his feet up on the table in front of the old stool. He stirred as I closed the door behind me and looked up at me, a startled expression on his face.

"Hi, Jim. What's new then?"

"Hello, Scabby, not much," I replied. "I just want a favour from you. I'll make it worth your while!"

"Sure, Jim. You name it!" he replied, shifting his feet down off the table. "Like a Coke?"

"Yes please!" I answered and he set two mugs up on the table and filled them both up.

"Here you are, Jim, help yourself! Now, what's this favour you're wanting?" He sat down opposite me, looking at me inquiringly.

I went on to explain to Scabby that I wanted a couple of cases of ·76mm shells dropped off about four miles down the road, at the site near where I had the Sherman tank hidden.

"Shit man! You mean to tell me you got one of the big Shermans stashed up some place?"

"Yeah, I have, Scabby. Got to have some defence in case them Gerries start dropping around! Problem is, I've got no ammo!" Scabby gulped down his Coke, staring at me in amazement.

"There ain't no Gerries going to be dropped here with half the U.S. Army here, Jim! This place is like a fortress!"

"Don't you believe it, Scabby! Them sods can drop in at anytime and I'm making sure I'm ready! I ain't relying on the Yanks to mop 'em up! Anyway, what the hell, Scabby, I just want a favour, not a lecture, and you're getting a few bottles of Scotch, so what?"

"Well, I don't know, Jim. If I get caught by them snowdrops (Military Police) with high explosives in my ambulance, I'll end up in Levenworth!"

"You ain't going to get stopped and searched, you silly bastard, especially when you're driving an ambulance, Scabby!" I replied. "It will only take you twenty minutes to get there, toss them off in the hedge on the corner of the wood, and then hightail it back here and say you got called out on a false alarm! You'll think of some excuse! Come on, there's four bottles in it for you, so what do you say?"

"Well, I guess that's simple enough." said Scabby, "but it's gonna be chancy loading them up, ain't it?"

"No, don't worry," I told him, "I'll drive the Studebaker 6x6 up round the back. It's got a whole load on. Meanwhile, bring yours round the back too and we'll throw the shells in and after dark, you drive out and meet me on the very top of Tidworth Hill dead on 7.00 p.m., anyway, I'll wait from 7.00 p.m. onwards, and you pick me up and I'll show you where to drop us off. You can be back here within an hour!"

"Okay, Jim. See you at seven and, by the way, how about the bottles, Jim?"

"I'll give you them tomorrow, Scabby. See you after tea then, but I'll go and get the truck. Move your ambulance round quick."

I went back over to the ammo truck and, after a few minutes, had transferred the shells into the ambulance and put the truck back on the parking lot. Then I made my way home for tea and to get ready for 7.00 p.m.!

Christ, what luck! I thought, as I sat eating my dinner. I was gulping it down fast, as I couldn't wait till seven. Just think, ammo at last! I just hope them Gerries don't land before I get my hands on it and get it loaded up on Herman, and at the weekend I'll drive it three miles over the firing ranges and get firing practice in. Sunday's best, there will be no Yanks up there. I don't want a shell up my arse, I thought!

I made my way up Tidworth Hill. It had started to rain. Better still, I thought, it will give us a bit more cover. I got to the top and waited for Scabby Norton. I knew he wouldn't keep me waiting, because he had to get the ammo off before his relief driver came on at 9.00 p.m. that night!

I looked at my watch, it was five after seven and no sign of Scabby. But, just a minute, there were some headlights and the sound of a motor labouring up the steep hill towards me. I strained my eyes, waiting for it to get closer, and soon, sure enough, Scabby pulled up where I stood. I ran round to the passenger side and opened the door.

"Quick, jump aboard, Jim!" he shouted, and off we went.

"You got out okay, then, Scabby?"

"Yeah, but I can't waste no time. I was shitting myself someone was going to call me out on an accident, with this load in the back!"

I directed him down to the edge of Collingbourne Woods and he pulled up where I wanted to drop the shells off.

"There you are, Scabby, grab that end!" and between us we unloaded the shells beneath the hedge. I covered them up with a little foliage and we both climbed back up into the cab.

"Just drop me near the village and you can get back!" I shouted.

Scabby started the motor and shoved her in gear and we started to move, but for only a few feet, then we got bogged down in the mud and no effort would shift us out!

"Stick her in four-wheel-drive, Scabby!" I shouted.

Scabby tried again, and after several tries, it was obvious we were getting in deeper to the axles!

"Jesus, Holy shit!" shouted Scabby, "now I really am in trouble! How in the hell am I going to get back to the Depot? I've got my relief coming in at nine!"

"Don't worry!" I replied, "it's only 7.45 and the best thing to get us out in quick time is for me to pull you out with the Sherman!" Scabby turned and stared at me in amazement.

"Why of course, Jim, go get it and let's get the hell out of here! Here, take my flashlight!"

I made my way up the narrow track into the woods. Herman was only a few minutes' walk away, and soon, in the beam of my lamp, I could see the dark shadow of the Sherman. I had to crank the motor over to break the oil seal out and, after a few minutes, I was sitting at the controls.

I switched on the panel lights and then the ignition. I pumped the Ki-gas a few times, turned to left magneto, squeezed both boost and starter switches and then came the whine as the motor turned over and very soon crackled into life.

Jesus, what a terrible noise! I kept the engine on a fast tickover to warm it up as quickly as possible, and opened my driver's hatch and in came the rain water, running down my back! I cranked the seat up, so I could see where I was driving and prepared to move off. I switched the lights on full power. The whole area in front of me was floodlit and I moved it down to where Scabby was sitting in his cab.

I decided to pull up close to him so I could pull him out with me reversing. I jumped down and ran up to his cab.

"Sit there, Scabby, I'll get her hooked up. You mustn't go back shitted up to the eyebrows!"

After a lot of work, I managed to get the hawser off the back of the tank and connect the U-bolts between the two vehicles. Soon we were ready. I climbed aboard Herman and gently dragged Scabby out onto harder ground, unhooked, and told Scabby to take off, as I'd make my own way back.

"Thanks a million, Jim. For a little guy, you sure are smart!" And he was gone into the night!

I dragged the roll of camouflage netting off the back of the tank and spread it out near the cases of ammo, pulled them all into the netting, hooked them on to the back-end and, carefully, dragged them back to my hideout up in the woods.

I didn't get home that night until midnight, but it was well worth it when I eventually climbed into bed that rainy evening!

CHAPTER 29

Wheelman Stanislaus Peschec

I FIRST met PFC Stanislaus Peschec at the army PX in the barracks at Perham Down one summer evening. I was watching a crap game between several GIs and his first words to me were: "Have you got any sisters, Limey?"

Peschec was a tall guy, lean and kind of mean-looking. I tried to avoid his conversation, but he persisted in his questions, trying to be friendly, I suppose, but I took an instant dislike to him. I told him I had no sisters and he asked me if I could arrange a meeting with a young lady for him.

"I'll give you five bucks, sonny, If you get me a blind date."

Christ, I thought, she would have to be blind to go out with him.

"Sorry, mate," I replied, laughing, "I don't know any gals that much, and you'd need to spend two grand on your face before any of the girls will go out with you round here. Why don't you go to one of the dances at the weekends in Andover?"

"Yes, I guess you're right, sonny!" he replied and shared the joke. "I come from Chicago. My folks were Polish. Came from Warsaw back in the early twenties. I was born on the goddam boat as she docked in the States!" Peschec went on and on, with me nodding or shaking my head as he poured out his life story.

"Here, have a Coke – what's your name?"

"Jim," I replied.

"Yeah, now," he went on, "I guess I've done every kinda job going, truck driver, washing up in restaurants, bellboy, and you'd never believe it, a chauffeur for a real live gangsters for about a year!" Peschec took out a bottle from a bag below the table and took several gulps. "Like a drop in your Cola, Jim?"

"No thanks, don't use it!" I answered.

"Aw, shit, try some!"

"No thanks, you go ahead."

Peschec continued with his life story. "I used to drive a guy named Big Sorbo, never knew his full name, but the pay was good. I used to be on call all hours. Shit! He'd phone me any hour of the day or night and we'd take off right across the States, sometimes driving for three days or more. I had the reputation as the best wheelman in Chicago, that's how Big Sorbo signed me up to drive for him!"

"What made you leave him if it was such a good job then, mate?"

"Don't call me mate. My name's Stanislaus, call me Stan. Well, the reason I left after about a year was that he started getting involved in bank stick-ups and one day we are outside a small bank, me at the wheel of this Packard, Big Sorbo in the back seat. He had sent in two of his hired guns to stick the place up and was hoping for big pickings. He was waiting to throw the back door open when they came running out with the loot. I was beginning to get edgy after months of driving him all over the place and already I had a couple of close shaves outside banks. I reckoned, secretly, that this would be my last bank job for him, I was planning to do a moonlight once I got a lot of dough, hightail it to the other side of the States and enlist in the army, as I had a strong feeling Big Sorbo wouldn't let me go easily! We sat there, it seemed like ages, but it had only been a minute or two, then what we dreaded most happened! A black-and-white (police car) slid down the road and parked about fifty yards ahead of us!"

Stan paused to take another slurp!

"Yeah, this black-and-white just down the road, and just then there was this gunfire from inside the bank! I started the motor. Big Sorbo opened the rear door in anticipation. Suddenly, his two guns came out of the bank. As they ran down the steps with a large carry-all – gunfire again – from inside the bank, I guess, and they both fell to the ground hit by bullets. As one of them fell he swung the bag over to where we were parked and it fell a few feet short of the door. Big Sorbo jumped out of the car and as he grabbed the bag and threw it ahead of him into the car, another shot was fired and Sorbo went down without a sound. I drove the car a few feet in reverse to slam the rear door, then shoved her in gear and took off down the street, being forced to leave Sorbo on the sidewalk. Just as I passed the black-and-white a cop stepped out and fired right at me. One slug went through by front screen and another through the rear. By now I was really shitting my pants, I couldn't stop, no sirree, I just put my foot on that gas pedal and hightailed it out of there. I made a few lefts and rights, got right down into the side streets as far away and as fast as I could. I had to dump this Packard pronto.

As I drove on in panic I wondered how much dough was in the bag in the back. I soon got to a disused warehouse yard pretty well concealed from the road, found a corner to hide the car, and skidded to a stop, wiped my fingerprints off everywhere possible and after grabbing the bag in the back walked casually away until I was far enough to stop and take a look in the bag. Jesus! It was packed with bills. I started to sweat. I've got to get out of town, I've got to hide this bag first, get a car and then pick up the dough and skedaddle out quick!

"I had an old pal I was sure I could rely on to sell me a car cheap, and keep his mouth shut. He lived about a mile away, and I went up to his apartment. After a few precautionary diversions I got to his place and rang his door-bell. My pal, Walt, opened the door. 'Hi, Stan! Come in, glad to see you.' I went in to his dingy room. Walt closed the door behind me and said he'd just heard on the news about the robbery, 'Your boss Sorbo is dead, so are the two guys who pulled the robbery. They say you got away with at least a hundred-and-twenty big ones, but they couldn't give a good description of the driver.' Look, Walt, I interrupted, I got to have a car tonight, a Pontiac if you can let me have yours. Can you sell it to me?"

" 'Sure, Stan, I can arrange that. Where's the dough?'

"I have hid it till dark, I'll pick it up later when I get a car. I'll see you okay for cash, Walt. How much do you want for the Pontiac?"

" 'Well look, Stan, that's mighty hot money! If you're figuring on using some of that to pay me, why don't we go and get the cash and come back here, and you stay here for a few days till things cool down a little. Hide out here, and I'll see my fence and get your cash laundered. But don't you think you wanna get it counted first? The radio flash said there was over a hundred-and-twenty thou'.'"

"Well, Jim, here I was with more money than I had ever dreamed of and here was Walt, the only guy who could identify me. I took a long look at Walt. I had known him a long time, I had to trust him. Anyway, I had no choice, had I?" Stan took another drink.

"I'll have to get home, Stan, it's getting late you know," I said.

"You got to get the punch line yet, Jim. Nearly finished. You can't miss the best bit of it!" Stan continued with his story.

"Yes, I guess I had to trust Walt as I was saying, so I agreed with Walt and after dark we drove up to the spot where I had hidden the bag of cash. We parked up and waited a few moments. There was no-one about and I jumped out of the car and went to the hiding place. I picked up the bag of money from behind a pile of litter in the corner of this empty shack and got back into the car, then Walt drove off back to his apartment. Soon we were counting the dough on the floor. We counted 90,650 dollars, not the 120,000 the radio had reported. Walt was putting some of the money in small bags and then we hid the lot in an air condition vent for the night.

Walt suggested we take the cash to his fence after talking to him on the phone, arguing over the price for changing it to clean money. I was to end up with only forty grand out of over ninety, but to me that was still a fortune and there was no way I could spend any of that hot money myself, was there Jim?

"So, that was that. Next day dear old Walt said he wouldn't be no more than two hours, so I settled down in the armchair with a double Scotch and feeling like a million bucks. I began making plans. I would give Walt a good price for his Pontiac, a few dollars for his trouble, and take off to Texas and keep out of sight for a while. Just then, the radio blared out the Pearl Harbor report and,within hours, we were at war with Japan and Germany!

Well, Jim, I guess I had one or two whiskies and next thing I'm waking up. Must have fell asleep. I looked at the time, it was twenty after three – Walt had been gone nearly six hours! Sweat was running down my back. Where in hell was Walt? I waited. Still no sign of him. It was now getting on for nine-thirty in the evening and I'm worried, man, am I worried about my dough!

I finally ended up going to bed at three the next morning, and Walt had not returned when I got up, either! Well, I had to face reality, Jim. Walt had run out on me with my dough, and I have not seen him since that day. If I ever meet up with him, I'll blow his head off!

I eventually sneaked down to 'Frisco and enlisted in the Infantry and here I am, still as broke as before!"

Stan leaned back in his chair and sighed: "Well, now you can tell your buddies you have met the best wheelman in Chicago!"

"A bit silly, trusting that Walt with your dough, weren't you?" I asked.

"Well, I guess so, Jim, but I had no option, did I? And I made a bad mistake! Perhaps it was just as well he did take the cash, because who knows where I'd be now. Maybe I could have started all over again, but I guess no good would have come out of it!"

"Well, Stan, nice to hear your life story, as short as it was, but don't you feel you are doing something really worthwhile fighting for your country?"

"You don't call this, sitting on my arse in England, fighting for my country do you, Jim?"

"Don't worry," I replied, "You'll get plenty of action soon enough. When you get some bloody great blond Gerries charging at you, that's when you'll see how much guts you got!"

"What do you know about blond Gerries, Jim? You haven't seen much life in this God-forsaken place, have you?"

"Look, Stan, let me tell you something. You may have been a big wheelman back in Chicago, but here you're just another GI, just a number! We've been fighting this war long before you came on the scene, and I've seen plenty of action. We've had plenty of air-raids round here. How long you been here, Stan?"

"Seven weeks," he replied.

"Seven weeks! Christ, you haven't been here long enough to shit yet!"

Stan was getting a bit shirty by now. He started to his feet and said, "well, Jim, nice to have talked to you. Maybe I'll see you again, eh?"

"Yes, maybe so," I replied.

Stan walked a little unsteadily as he left the PX. I never saw him again. I heard, later, that he had gone absent without leave and, to my knowledge, he was never found.

I went home, as it was getting late, and as I arrived Dad was about to lock up.

"You late again, Jim!" he said.

"I've been talking to some Polish Yank in the PX, Dad. He's going to win the war all by his bloody self!"

"Come on, Jim, get to bed. We have to be up early in the morning. It's going to be a busy day."

"What's on then, Dad?"

"I've got to send out a big convoy tomorrow, so I'll call you early. Goodnight, son."

"Goodnight, Dad."

CHAPTER 30

Destination Braishfield

I HAD met a girl in Andover last Saturday. Her name was Betty. She was fifteen-years-old and she lived in Braishfield, near Romsey. I arranged to go over on Sunday, tomorrow, to her home for dinner and I would have to dress up in my army cadet uniform and 'borrow' a Jeep from Tidworth Hill where there were hundreds of brand new ones lined up. If I got up early I could get one away and use it for the day and return it late at night. I would have to watch out for the U.S. Military Police, as there were always plenty driving about in Jeeps or on motorcycles. Anyway, tomorrow I would chance my arm and have a go. He who dares, wins, my brother Bob used to tell me.

Sunday dawned, a rainy day, and I left home at nine o'clock and on the way through the village I passed Ethel Bowman coming out of the paper shop. I went on past the new school, past Brimstone Bottom and in the distance I could see the U.S. Army vehicles all lined up for miles, hundreds of them, of all types, including Jeeps. I kept my head down and made for the Jeep with sidescreens and tested the tank for gasoline, folded my forage cap down and sat in the driver's seat, ready to make a fast getaway!

I looked about and all seemed quiet. I would have to make my way across to Tidworth and then over to Stockbridge, on to Kings Somborne, then Motisfont, Michelmarsh and, finally, Braishfield.

I turned on the ignition, full choke, pressed the starter and the engine started. Soon I was away, up and then down Tidworth Hill and finally I arrived at Stockbridge. As I was coming into the thirty limit I saw two American Military Police, sitting astride their Harleys at the bottom of the hill, on the grass verge. By now, the rain had stopped, and I slowed down to a legal speed. The two MPs were now staring in the direction of my approach and one put his hand up for me to stop, trying to look the part!

Now, I had two options here. One, to stop and chance being caught or, give them a run for their money, over these wet roads (and I knew them better than the Yanks) I could lose them. I had nearly a full tank of gas and I could, with a bit of luck, get away. I decided to have a lark with them. I pulled up alongside the parked Harleys, opposite one of the MPs, but kept the engine running and engaged first gear. The MP nearest shouted across: "You got a trip ticket, buddy?"

"Vot you say Mein Herr?" I queried! The expression on his face changed to one of disbelief.

"Shit, Hey, you, get out of that goddam Jeep!" he shouted, as he scrambled to get his ·45 Colt out of its holster!

"See you in Berlin, Fritz!" I shouted back and roared away across the road and up the hill, keeping my head well down, and expecting a bullet to come ripping into the Jeep! I took a quick glance behind me and, sure enough, the two MPs were starting up their motorcycles.

'Oh boy, will this be good,' I thought, 'we'll see how good they are at riding. I hope they can't shoot too straight!'

Foot hard down, I capped the top of the steep hill and was away along the hill and winding road toward King Somborne. Within a minute or two, I could see two white helmets behind me, over the top of the hedge, speeding up fast, with sirens wailing! Wait till they come down to the bottom of the hill in Kings Somborne, there's a sharp right-hander and I'll probably lose them both!

It started to rain again. Ah, just the job, that'll slow them down! I belted down into Kings Somborne, taking extreme care on the blind corner by the green, swung right and on through the village and up the winding hill out on to the Romsey road. No need to take any diversions yet, I thought, and looked behind. Sure enough . . . Then there was only one! One down, one to go! One had, undoubtedly, slid off on the bend by the green, as it was a notoriously sharp bend, but his mate kept on coming! I got onto the straight and pushed my foot to the floor, then, CRASH! The righthand windscreen went! A positive bullet-hole in the corner! The sod's shooting at me! A canvas cover was not much protection from a ·45 heavy automatic pistol, so I had to think very quick! This guy can't take a joke!

I started to zig-zag where I could. I had to get rid of this guy, quickly! But how! The road was quiet but the rain was worse and I took another glance behind. The remaining MP had dropped back quite a bit, then, suddenly, he stopped and was soon lost from my view. He must have run out of guts!

I pressed on, expecting a road block but, keeping a good look out and looking behind, could see no sign of the MP. Just a few miles to go now and soon I would arrive at Betty's for lunch. I drove up the narrow road which led to the cottage where she lived, parked the Jeep well off the road out of sight, and took off my cap and walked up to her side door. She opened it and asked me in to the living room, where her mum sat knitting.

"Mum, this is Jim, the friend I told you about." Her mum was a slightly-built woman with a kindly face. I shook her small hand.

"Pleased to meet you, Madam."

"Pleased to meet you, Jim. You found us all right? It's a bad day for you driving. Is that an army car you've got?" she went on.

"Yes, U.S. Army! My Dad lent it to me to come out in. He's in charge at Tidworth and even though I'm only 14 I've got special licence to drive in wartime!"

"That's nice," she said. "Anyway, sit down and tell me all about yourself and family. Get Jim a cup of tea, Betty, look after your guest now!" she said, smiling. Betty went off to the kitchen and her mum turned to me. "My husband's away you know, in the navy."

"Oh, yes," I replied. The house was spotlessly clean and cosy, and soon Betty came back with the cups of tea.

"Dinner won't be long," she said, "Do you like rabbit pie?" Christ, I thought, as if I had seen enough rabbits . . .!

"Oh – yes, my favourite that, Betty!"

Later on her mum started to serve up the dinner and the rabbit pie was done to a turn. I sat back and looked out across the road to where the Jeep was.

"Things look bad for us in the war, Jim, don't they?" Betty went on, "Will we win, do you think?"

"Course we will!" I stated, "The Germans don't stand a chance, now the Yanks are here!"

"I'm not too keen on them Yanks," Betty's mother interrupted. "I suppose they're all right in their own country, but they boast a lot. Don't you think so, Jim?"

"Well, yes, I suppose so, but then that's just their way. They come from a large country and think that we're all yokels here. They're so used to everything on a big scale. Big time stuff, you know! Do you mind if I smoke?"

"No, go on, I don't mind, Jim," replied Betty's mum.

"Yes, they are really okay when you get to know them. You see I work with them and I have got to know their ways. They are trigger-happy mind you, but they are used to shooting a lot out there in America."

"Now, you go and sit in the other room and chat to Betty. After all, you did come over to see her, didn't you?"

Betty took me into the other room. There was a lovely large log fire burning and we sat down on the settee together, our fingers touching gently, as I reached my hand across to hers. Betty was a lovely, gentle girl. We sat talking all the afternoon long and then had tea.

Soon the night became dark and I began to dread the drive back to Tidworth Hill, as every MP in the area had, probably, been alerted to keep a watch out for the Jeep!

185

I thanked Betty's mum for the lovely hospitality and we walked out to the Jeep. Her mum waved from the door. "Hope to see you soon, Jim. Come any time." What that, she went into the house. I took Betty in my arms and kissed her gently on the lips. I knew I would probably never see her again. I had that feeling!

"Thanks for coming, Jim," she murmured, "have a safe ride home." If only she knew!

I started the Jeep and headed out to the main road, the special black-out headlights, with their pencil beam, lighting the country road as I cautiously drove on into the night. However, the drive back to the army park was uneventful and I turned off the lights just before I got there and quietly parked the Jeep up on the end of the rows of vehicles. I got out, quietly, and was about to walk away when, out of the darkness, a voice said: "Halt! or I fire!"

I froze for a moment. Now I've had it, I thought, but I was determined to brazen it out. I shouted back: "Listen, bud, I've just been out for a ride and I haven't done any harm to the Jeep. I live around here, so let's call it leaselend, eh, and forget it!"

"You ain't go no authority to be driving none of United States property, have you? Step forward over here, bud, and don't make any false move!" he roared.

It was pitch dark, so I was sure he couldn't see me and I took a chance. I slid down between the rows of Jeeps and shouted back: I'll tell you something, bud, I can see you and you can't see me. You mentioned shooting first but I'll tell you this much, I've got a bead on you, you stupid sod with that cigarette of yours stuck in your face! How about if I was a German? You would be a dead duck! I've got a grease-gun here and if you fancy a dust-up with the fastest gun in Wiltshire, just fire the first shot! Get me?" I saw the cigarette stub go flying!

"I don't believe this!" he shouted.

"You had better believe it, mate!" I shouted back.

"Listen, Limey. Just get your arse out of here, pronto, I have only to blow my whistle and my buddies will be here. So take off!"

"Yeah. Okay, I'm going, mate!"

I made my way back, cautiously, down the line, keeping my head well down, until I knew it would be safe to get up and run like hell. I took a long round-about way back home and there the day's adventure ended.

I had better slack off a bit, I thought. Things are getting a bit too hot for comfort, and my luck can only last so long. I've had more than my fair share, up to now!

CHAPTER 31

A Sojourn at Wokefield Park

MY luck finally ran out one day, when I had been out shooting hares with Dad's Home Guard Lee Enfield rifle. On this particular day, I was over near the polo field and was firing at three hares, which I desperately wanted to shoot for a local butcher. It was a fairly windy day and, in my haste to shoot them all, they suddenly split up and headed away in different directions. This caused me to throw my usual caution to the winds and I was shooting rapidly, and haphazardly in various directions. Then, unfortunately, I decided to concentrate my fire on one which was heading, unknown to me then, in the direction of some farmworkers, who were loading a farm cart on the other side of the hill. Apparently, a few of my bullets had ricocheted off the cart and made them scatter for cover!

Meanwhile, I had hit the hare and ran up to where it lay. As I made my way back with it to the village, I was suddenly confronted by the local constabulary and a couple of farmworkers!

Well, I was caught, bang to rights! No excuse this time! Here I stood, rifle slung over my shoulder, a loaded bandoleer of ·303 ammunition, and a dead hare in my hand!

"Where did you get that hare, then, Jimmy?" said the gloating constable, knowing he had really copped me this time!

"It's been stalking me all day!" I replied, cockily, "So I shot it in self-defence!"

"Ha! Ha! very funny!" he scoffed, "Clever cock, eh? Well, you give me that rifle and all them bullets and let's go back to the Police Station!" I handed him the Enfield and bullets and off we went.

This time, the law decided they could do with a break from any antics, so they sent me off to lovely Berkshire. Between Mortimer and Burfield was Wokefield Park, where a beautiful old country mansion was being used as a home for naughty boys. It was administered by the Brothers of De la Salle, all Irish and Catholic. Some of the Brothers were under thirty years of age and, despite their order, were tough guys too! As I found out later!

I stepped off the train at Mortimer and was taken to Wokefield Park, which had been renamed 'St. Benedict's School'. I walked through the main entrance by the lodge and up the very long winding gravel road which led up to the front door of this beautiful house. I must say, my thoughts were rather confused. I could not understand why this large house was being used for us wayward lads. I soon found out besides sporting over a hundred beds, a lake, and sports field. St. Benedict's School had workshops for joinery and plumbing, instructors for gardening and a substantial farming industry, controlled by a manager who really got results from the acres of farmland of Wokefield Park.

Upon arrival I was ushered into the office of the Head Brother, who's name was Brother Bruno. I sat down opposite him across a large oak desk, his piercing blue eyes looking me up and down. Brother Bruno was around seventy-eight years of age and he started by asking me by name, age, the usual things and went on to give me a pep-talk. He had been reading a sheaf of papers in front of him, which must have been concerning my case history. He didn't seem very impressed!

"You need God's guidance very urgently, my son!" he said, "You have lost your way somewhat!" he went on. I was thinking, I sure had lost my way, ending up in this place. What a come-down for me, I thought, as I sat there, listening to Brother Bruno reading me out all the do's and don'ts and what the penalty was for disobedience of these rules. I assured him I would stay on the right side of God, and away I went down to the hall to meet the other boys.

There were about one hundred and twenty boys in this place, aged between 13 years to about 17 years. Most were from London. I was given a 'uniform' consisting of a rough cotton shirt, short knee-length trousers and an old army battledress tunic, which had been dyed blue, heavy socks and boots completed the issue. I also learned that I would get about 2/6d a week pocket-money! Some come-down from the previous 'high-life' I had been used to!

Soon it was teatime. We all sat at long tables in the dining room which, in the early days had been the large study. I went to my allotted seat. There were about six of us lads at each table. All the boys were staring at me as I sat down for my tea, making remarks like "Down with the Yanks' etc.", as word had spread quickly that I had been working with the U.S. Army. I ignored all the shouts and got on with my tea.

"I'm Bryan James," said the mouth opposite me. "I'm from Hackney. Take no notice of them. I'll show you the ropes. After tea we go down to the yard for two hours recreation and I'll introduce you to a few of my mates!"

After tea we went down for recreation and, as I arrived in the large cobblestone yard, all the boys were standing, or sitting around, smoking and eagerly waiting for me to join them. Bryan took me by the arm.

"Here, Jim. Let's sit here and don't give all your fags away. If anyone asks, say you have only a couple left!"

Now, the general procedure was that when a new boy arrived, he took on the 'cock' of the school in the boxing ring in the gym. This served as an entertainment for everyone and the Brothers turned a blind eye, as long as you used boxing gloves, and one of them refereed the match, which was one round, lasting until one threw in the towel, or dropped!

Bryan nudged my arm. "See that crowd sitting over there? Se that tall, thin, blond-haired one? He's the cock of the school."

They were all looking over in my direction and, soon, one of them came over to me and sneered, "Taffy wants to know if you'll have him out!" I looked over at Taffy. He was glaring at me, hands on his hips, as though to say "are you yellow?"

"Well," I replied, "I don't fight, my Mum don't like me fighting really!" and they all roared laughing.

Taffy's courage brewed up at that remark and he ambled over.

"You're not cissy are you, Yank?" (From that time on the name stuck while I was at the school.)

"Well, it's not that," I replied, "only you are bigger than me and, after all, you are the cock of the school, aren't you?"

"That's correct," he retorted, "and, another thing, if you're afraid of fighting me, okay, just make sure you give me five Woodbines every Friday!"

"I'd rather fight out, Taffy!" I replied, calmly.

He swung round as he was walking away, surprised, his face crimson. Everyone started shouting "Fight, Fight" and began stampeding towards the gym for ringside seats. Brother Ignatious was on duty at the time. This was nothing new to him and in he went to referee the match.

Bryan walked in with me and a few lads who wanted me to win were giving me little bits of advice on how to keep out of trouble when fighting Taffy!

We stripped down to the waist and stood in our corners. The boxing ring was elevated slightly and the crowd hushed whilst Brother Ignatious read the rules.

Taffy was a mean-looking fellow. He was lean and looked as hard as nails. I had made up my mind that I was not going to go any distance. I was going to smash into him from the start. No dancing around for me. I was an extremely fast one-two merchant, but no-one knew that, yet!

On went the gloves and shouts like "Don't kill him, Taffy," filled the gym. I was quickly sizing up Taffy. He was taller than me by, maybe, six inches, but I had the better physique, and I knew he was going to start by prancing about the ring.

Time! Brother blew his whistle! We both jumped up, Taffy came out to the centre of the ring, pursing his lips like he wanted to give me a big kiss, and snorting through his nose like a racehorse, his long arms pumping up and down, but his guard too low! I came out, southpaw, slowly and circled him. The gym was silent in anticipation.

Then Taffy charged, swinging as he came, and I quickly sidestepped and he missed me completely. Everyone roared laughing. Taffy turned round, fuming. Still wanting to kiss me and snorting harder, he made a few stabs with his left, but I blocked and rode them. He charged again, and missed. The gym was in an uproar and, suddenly, I could hear a lot of voices changing sides. "Come on Yank!" I must nail him I thought. His flurries were getting too close for comfort!

As he came in once more I stood firm and gave him the one-two about six times in rapid succession. He fell back and I followed up with lightning blows. He retreated to the ropes and I still pounded him. Suddenly, he went to his knees. The whistle went.

"Step back, Yank." shouted Brother.

I stepped back. Taffy's eyes were wild as he looked up and Brother made him wipe his gloves as he got to his feet, and blew the whistle.

"Box on!"

I went in before he could recover and punched him to the corner. My blood was up now. Cock of the school, eh? I thought. Crash! Bang! Wallop! He was down again, taking one straight left to the side of his head. I heard his teeth rattle!

Brother blew his whistle again. "Step back!" he shouted, and asked Taffy if he'd had enough! Taffy nodded. "Shake hands!" ordered Brother and, reluctantly, he shook my hand and said: "Christ, you're fast, Yank!"

The cheers were deafening. They carried me outside and, as was the custom after a fight, dumped me, and later Taffy, into the showers – cold!

Eventually, I dried off and came out into the yard. All the lads were milling around me and some of Taffy's old pals had changed sides. "Where did you learn to box?" they asked. "Will you be my wax, mate?" (close friend – share everything) they were saying. After a time, Taffy came over and shook hands again.

"Well, mate, I've met some tough guys down on the docks in Cardiff, but I've met my match tonight!" Thereafter, Taffy turned out to be a good friend to me until, tragically, he was found hanging from a curtain cord some months later. The poor fellow had come from a broken home and had been pushed them pillar to post all his young life, and found suicide the only want out of the hardship he had endured.

The weeks were going by and one day Sgt Single visited me in his Jeep with a couple of his buddies. He brought me cigarettes and candies. I was allowed to spend two hours talking over old times and was sorry when they had to say goodbye.

Life was very very healthy, if not hard, at St. Benedict's. I got on very well with the boys and the staff and kept the cars and farm tractors in good running order. I was in peak physical condition.

The annual sports day soon arrived and I was the fastest 100 and 200 yards sprinter in the area. I beat the runners from nearby Bradfield College. Life was enjoyable, but I missed my family and, of course, my friends in the Depot at Tidworth.

I was never reprimanded at any time during my stay at St. Benedict's. I used to play the organ at Mass at weekends, and gradually, my life seemed to take a settled course.

Then came the day when I was told "you are free to go home," and I said my goodbyes and got on the train in Reading, back to Ludgershall.

What would it be like back in the village, I thought, after all these months.

The war was just ending as I arrived home. Most of the U.S. Army had departed. All my buddies will have gone, perhaps. Some had been killed in France in the Second Front. After the fast life I had spent since the beginning of the war, what would it be like in peacetime!

I arrived home to find my Dad about to buy a garage business in Ludgershall. A few of my American friends were still in Tidworth, about to leave for home. I knew, as I said my final goodbyes to them, that this would be the end of a wonderful adventure. The good times, the scrapes I had got into, the wonderful friends I had made were about to become a memory and, looking back, it seemed I had dreamed a wonderful, impossible dream, but it had all happened to me.

I had done all these things, met all these great guys, lived an unbelievable adventurous life in those few short years. Could I ever look back on my childhood days and regret one thing? Regret I was a boy in these war-torn years? Never! I am glad I lived and survived the war. Many of my dear friends would never come back, ever!

To the GIs who, like Father Kelly and Colonel Richland and many, many others, who gave a lot of their advice and time to me, a mere slip of a lad they met when they left their homeland, to give aid to us in our hour of need – I say "thanks a million!"

I stood at the army barracks' main gate and watched my last few friends depart for their ships down at Southampton. The drivers of the trucks started their motors and, one by one, they pulled out of the camp. They waved their hands to me as they roared past.

"So long, Jimmy!" some shouted. Others, "Come over and see us someday!" I waved back, tears streaming down by cheeks unashamedly. So this is how it is, I thought. It seemed like my life was at an end.

I never saw any of them again. Had this really been a dream after all? I thought, as I walked back down Station Road.

I recalled the time when I first saw the troop-train steaming into Ludgershall, carrying those magnificent men. What happened after that, happened to me!

My back was now turned, forever, on those few years of great adventure. No one person could have had, and would never know, such a thrilling experience. I knew, at that moment, peace had returned to England, our green and pleasant land!

CHAPTER 32

Biddesden House Revisited

THE date was 17th October 1986 and this was the day of my visit to Biddesden House after a gap of forty-odd years. Lord Moyne and his wife Elisabeth had graciously permitted me to visit them and see the house of which I recalled so many happy moments all those years ago.

For late autumn on this Sunday morning, the sun was unusually warm. I was just five minutes' driving time from Biddesden and, as I drove along the country lane, I passed the field where I had, as a lad, built my plane. Cattle now grazed there serenely and trees had grown wildly, they were only seedlings in 1942. It felt was though I was stepping back in time.

I turned into the long and impressive drive at Biddesden House and, as the house came into view, my heart missed a beat. At first glance it seemed to me that nothing had changed and, really, I had not wanted it to.

It was then, in the distance, that I saw Lady Moyne, standing near the front door. Her hair was streaked with grey, but the years had been kind to he. It was not difficult to remember her as the lovely person with the beautiful dark hair and disarming smile, and I recognised her immediately. I shook her hand as she greeted me and, after a few words, we walked into the large hall. Lady Moyne pointed to the large painting of General Webb on the wall.

"I suppose you remember him, don't you, James?"

"Yes, I do," I replied. Little did she know I struggled hard to keep back a tear!

I then met several members of her family, including young Luke, her grandson, who thought nothing of mowing the large lawns on the big motor mower, before lunch. This was no mean feat as he was only eight years of age! I immediately felt the warmth and happiness within these walls. There was nothing artificial, I felt at ease, it seemed to come naturally in this happy place.

Finally, we all moved into the dining room, where we all sat down to a beautiful lunch and the conversation rotated mostly around the war-time years. I had not seen Lord Moyne for almost forty-five years. He knew my father well and my Dad held him in high esteem. I looked closely at this man who was faultless in character and loved by all who had the privilege of knowing him.

Only too soon the time came for me to leave, as I had a long night drive back to Liverpool. I tried to savour the last few moments, then when I had said my goodbyes and as I drove down the long drive, I consciously glanced over my shoulder to the place on the lawn and thought back to that evening years ago, when I saw the phantom Lady gliding across on that moonlit night.

No! I couldn't see her, but I knew she was, perhaps, bidding me farewell!

Biddesden House. (Photo: Courtesy Lord Moyne)

CHAPTER 33

Reunion at Castletown House

I WAS going to visit the Honourable Desmond Guinness, who I had not met for over forty years. Desmond had invited me to spend the day at his home in Leixlip, County Kildare, not far from the fair city of Dublin. He lived in this beautiful Leixlip Castle, which was in pristine condition, with a long winding drive leading up to the magnificent tower. I was impressed! What a lovely home!

It was a lovely September day. On my arm was the girl I loved, Sheila, my wife. I gripped her hand in mine. It was so fine to have her with me on this very happy occasion.

As we walked up and turned the corner, we came upon this grand view. Desmond was always someone special to me and after so many years, I wondered to myself if he had changed very much. Would I recognise him?

It was then I heard his voice calling my name from where he stood across the paddock. My heart missed a beat! Then he was walking down towards us leading a lovely mare. As he came close I could see it was really him.

"Hello James! Nice to see you again after all these long years!" We shook hands, warmly and I introduced Sheila, then we all walked off towards the Castle.

"Come and meet the family," he said.

We entered by the front door, and he introduced us to his lovely wife and children. We were now in the spacious drawing room. How many of the famous and infamous had trod here in years gone by? This room was, in fact, the base of a huge tower of this very imposing castle.

After a while we were called for lunch and sat around a beautiful scrubbed wooden table in the kitchen, and enjoyed an appetising meal.

"Now, Jim and Sheila," said Desmond, "you must see Castletown House* at Celbridge, only two miles down the river. I will drive you down there and we will spend the afternoon there."

Needless to say, I had no idea what was coming. Desmond had not told me he also owned the largest house in Ireland, which had a great history, dating back to the time when erection began in 1722. In order to try to convey to the interested reader, the beauty and splendour of this

---

* Castletown House: Largest house in Ireland (*Guinness Book of Records*).

Lord and Lady Moyne 50 years on. (Photo: Courtesy Lord Moyne)

mansion, I will set down a little of its history, which I, personally, felt very moving and which left me, not a little, awe-inspired!

Castletown was the first great stone Palladian mansion in Ireland, which was built to correct classical proportions. Work began in the year 1722, making it contemporary with Mereworth in England. The house is well documented in many respects, but the architect had been, for many years, a mystery. It has now been established beyond doubt that Castletown House was designed by none other than the Italian architect Allesdro Galilei, whose best-known work was the facade he added to the old Basilica of St John in Lateran, Rome. In fact the central block of Castletown, with its facade of 'stupendous monotony' is essentially that of an Italian town palace.

After lunch Desmond drove us down to Castletown. Soon we were through the main entrance and the one-and-a-half mile long drive to the house loomed ahead. It seemed like we would never get there. I would hate the walk on a cold, dark night, I thought!

"Here we are, Jim," said Desmond, as we came up to the front entrance and stopped on the gravel drive. "Now let me show you round and I'll explain the history, or some of it, to you as we walk around." I stood by the car and looked up at this magnificent place, truly fit for a prince!

Desmond bought this house in 1967 and it is now the headquarters of the Irish Georgian Society, of which Desmond is president, and was the first country house in Ireland to open its doors to the public. William Connolly was the builder, known as 'Speaker Connolly' as he was elected Speaker of the Irish House of Commons in 1715, only relinquishing shortly before his death in 1729. He was acknowledged to be the richest commoner in Ireland, starting life as the son of a publican in Ballyshannon, Co. Donegal. He later amassed his fortune dealing in forfeited estates. He liked to be known as plain Mr Connolly of Castletown.

He had married Katherine Conyngham. They had no children, and his widow lived alone in the great house for twenty-three years. In 1740 she built a remarkable eye-catcher to close the vista to the rear of Castletown. The famous landmark, known as the Connolly Folly. She built it to give employment, as great hardship had resulted from the severe winter of 1739. She was a very caring and charitable woman, it seems, and often said that she would like to die looking at her beautiful house from her chair on the lawn, where she often sat with her friends taking tea on fine days. It was in that chair, fittingly, that she passed away in 1752.

After a passage of many years, the house then became almost derelict and it was eventually bought by Desmond.

The history, the views, the beauty of the architecture is far too vast to cover in my story but, nevertheless, it made a great and lasting impression on me in the short time I was honoured to grace its corridors. Here was a mansion I would one day, surely, return to with my family. A true jewel in Ireland's crown of beauty.

After three hours, Desmond must have been exhausted and had to leave us on an urgent appointment. We stood, once again, on the steps of this great house and said our farewells.

Sheila and I walked back down that long drive to the imposing gates in the far distance and made our way back to Dublin for our trip back to Liverpool.

After 60 years on this earth I am still a boy at heart! Deep within me, dormant, and impatient to breathe again the breath of those vibrant years, lies the boy whose life certainly was a many-splendoured thing!

Castletown House, Celbridge, Co. Kildare, built 1722. Headquarters of the Irish Georgian Preservation Society. (Photo: Courtesy The Hon. Desmond Guinness)

The Hon. Desmond Guinness, aged sixty. Circa 1991. (Photo: Courtesy The Hon. Desmond Guinness)

The Guinness Book of Records
Personal Aviation Records

PILOTS – Youngest
"A wholly untutored James A. Stoodley, aged 14 years 5 months, took his 13-year-old brother John on a twenty-nine minute joy ride in an unattended U.S. Piper Cub Trainer near Ludgershall, Wiltshire, in December 1942." – *Courtesy The Guinness Book of Records.*

James Stoodley, a Wiltshire-born man, has resided in Liverpool since the early 1950s, married a Liverpool girl and raised seven children (two boys and five girls). He is now a retired motor engineer.

For information on further copies write to:
James A. Stoodley, 26 Agar Road, Liverpool L11 8NQ, England.
Tel.: 051 256 5904

Extract from The Guinness Book of Records 1994
Copyright © Guinness Publishing Limited 1993